THE
Divine Magnet

THE
Divine Magnet

HERMAN MELVILLE'S
Letters to **NATHANIEL HAWTHORNE**

edited with an introduction by
MARK NIEMEYER

foreword by
PAUL HARDING

The Divine Magnet:
Herman Melville's Letters to Nathaniel Hawthorne

Orison Books, Inc.
PO Box 8385
Asheville, NC 28814
www.orisonbooks.com

ISBN-13: 978-0-9906917-5-4 (paper)
ISBN-13: 978-0-9906917-6-1 (e-book)

Distributed to the trade by Itasca Books
1 (800) 901-3480
www.itascabooks.com

Cover art by Claire Bateman and Kiah Ann Bellows (acrylic and ink on paper; collage)

Cover design and layout by Matthew Mulder

Manufactured in the U.S.A.

ORISON
BOOKS

TABLE OF CONTENTS

FOREWORD

by Paul Harding

MOST WRITERS stand in awe of Herman Melville. Melville's prose fills the English language to near bursting. It is righteous, huge, thunderously beautiful, and delivered with the gusto of an Old Testament prophet. It obliterates every tame writing workshop rule by which any scribbler has ever felt tyrannized. Who, for example, has ever objected to *Moby-Dick* being written in first person omniscient?

Best of all, Melville's writing is gracious—large-spirited and noble because each of his magnificent sentences—all creation hung up from pole to pole, spinning on its axis, generating vast, gorgeous electro-magnetic fields of meaning—is devoted to commemorating the humblest lives. As he writes to Nathaniel Hawthorne in one of the following letters, he is "a mortal who boldly declares that a thief in jail is as honorable a personage as Gen. George Washington."

Close your eyes and fan through any of Melville's writings—the book at hand; *Moby-Dick*; the South Seas tales; one of his later, somewhat overcooked works, like the bizarre *Pierre*; or *The Confidence-Man*. Stop at any page. Stab your finger at any sentence and you will find the universe stretched across God and the devil, grace and cursedness, hope and despair, humanity spiraling and striving in between, and Melville in its midst, applying his genius to rescue the most hapless souls within from oblivion. Nearly every word Melville wrote can be read as recognition of the unfortunates fallen by the wayside or tossed overboard.

In other words, Melville's writing is supremely democratic. If the thief in jail or the swabbie clinging to the topmast shroud of a whaler is collared to the very *fiat lux* of this universe, it means that he belongs to this existence as much as any king, judge, or admiral. That swabbie can trace his ancestry back to the original particle from which we all exploded, all came forth, our earth an ark on the floodtide of dimensions, coming to teeter on an Ararat peak in our little bandwidth of existence, our single, tiny family huddled together on our tiny, fleeting planet, warmed by our tiny star, and he a fully vested citizen of such majesties.

If my metaphors sound particularly cosmic, they are attempted under the inspiration of Melville. It is this very kind of inspiration that Nathaniel Hawthorne, in person and in his collection *Mosses from an Old Manse*, gave Melville in the middle of trying to wrangle his white whale into its most monumental expression. In his famous review of the *Mosses*, Melville spends much space comparing Hawthorne to Shakespeare, in precisely the democratic spirit I've been describing. At the same time, he happened to be writing a book that is today held in a degree of reverence nearly equal to that reserved for Shakespeare. A difference between Melville's attitude to Shakespearean greatness and ours is that he claims it for a peer and in doing so gives himself the courage to attempt it for himself. He makes such genius accessible to the ambition of any person at all who might wish to attempt it.

One quality that ignited Melville's passion for Hawthorne and his art was a particular sort of darkness that he perceived in Hawthorne's stories. Hawthorne's work embodied, "a certain tragic phase of humanity . . . the tragicalness of human thought in its own unbiased, native, and profounder workings." It captured "the visible truth," by which Melville meant "the apprehension of the absolute condition of present things as they strike the eye of the man who fears them not, though they do their worst to him." In *Clarel*, he calls this "The natural language of the eye." The deepest truths can be discerned with the naked eye and are therefore available to every living soul. Freely approached, without fear, their darkness is revealed as a higher order of beauty.

Melville describes that darkness that so electrifies and galvanizes him in Hawthorne as a lingering trace of the "blue Calvinism" of Hawthorne's ancestors. Hawthorne is commonly understood to have rejected wholesale the Puritanism of his forebears, but what of Calvinism Melville detected in the *Mosses* might be seen as the conservation of what Hawthorne found best in that inheritance and a criticism of the worst. Inside that darkness is the authentic germ of a deep and abiding cosmology Melville himself preserved and renewed, in its original biblical idiom, as he agonized over matters of belief. It strikes at the deepest meaning and beauty of Melville's art that there is barely a page of his writing that does not make explicit reference to a character or story from the Bible.

That a non-believer, a figure for instance embodied in *Moby-Dick* by the glorious pagan harpooner Queequeg sitting in a swamped whaleboat during a howling storm, in the black of night, lost at sea, holding up a lit lantern in the maelstrom nevertheless, on the scant chance the *Pequod* might glimpse it and come to the rescue, "the sign and symbol of a man without faith, hopelessly holding up hope in the midst of despair;" that such a figure can be epitomized in the biblical language inherited by Shakespeare and Melville and Hawthorne speaks at the very least to that tradition's deep capaciousness, to its, we might well say, democratic embrace of both the saints and no-hopers, too, without any inconsistency of its own deepest premises. The term used in that tradition to describe this phenomenon is grace.

Today we writers are more apt to be embarrassed by the thought of such artistic aspirations, perhaps precisely because they are expressed in the idiom of holiness, of the sacred, of grace, and confine ourselves to the dreariness of mere virtuosity or fashionable blamelessness. Part of the source of that embarrassment is traceable to the success of the project of convincing many otherwise brilliant people that religion, so called, in any and all of its particulars and generalities, is to be avoided at all costs, superstitious, primitive, deeply unhip thing that it is. Don't open that Bible; you're liable to catch a case of stupid. It is easy to forget that censorship is an equal opportunity affliction, self-censorship especially. The fact that this proscription is so pervasive in certain influential circles these days speaks to an unsettling intellectual passivity in our thinkers and artists. It indicates an alarming obedience to authority, a lack of independent curiosity and imagination, a lack of simple piss and vinegar. How many writers withhold from their thought the very aesthetic and narrative traditions that make Melville's books the objects of their admiration? The difference is everything, because the greatness of Melville's ambition and his desire to point it out in Hawthorne's work and to discuss it with Hawthorne in person—he calls their talks together their "ontological heroics"—is precisely its democratic impulse, which is precisely expressed in the yoking of the idea of the divine or the sacred to the lives of "unlettered" Ishmael, for example, or poor Pip, his tambourine gone quiet, gaping at the abyss, his lot lamented as eloquently as that of any prince, in the finest language available to anyone. A fundamental element of Melville's art is the deliberate act of making such language available to people who, in what we by convenience call the real world, are perennially denied the dignities of literacy and self-determination. A deckhand gave us *Moby-Dick*. Melville calls writing it "ditcher's work" at one point. It is by bringing the frankly sacred into the ditch, though, that he activates the realms of beauty we so admire.

None of this requires any specifically religious inclination. The Bible is literature and ponders truth as such. Its contents are not confirmable scientifically or archeologically or even historically because they are literary and not scientific or archeological or historical. Attempting to refute religious ideas explored in stories and poems and songs according to scientific criteria is a categorical mistake so elementary its persistence can only be attributed to brute tendentiousness or simple idiocy. The truths of the Flood narrative depend for their confirmation as little upon unearthing Noah's ark in eastern Turkey as *Moby-Dick* does on finding a true plank of the *Pequod*. If the repositories of Western thought and wisdom prior to, say, Nagasaki and Hiroshima are largely expressed in theological—which is after all to say largely aesthetic, poetic, and narrative terms—our confession or rejection of any given denomination is irrelevant, at least in the face of this fact as fact. If we asked Ralph Waldo Emerson whether he forsook the God of his Calvinistic fathers, he might well tell us that he left the pulpit to pursue Him with all the greater vigor, while the church went into moral and spiritual decline in the opposite direction. Which is to say, his account might be that it was not he who rejected the heart of his own religion but the church. If we granted him his own terms, we might see him illuminated suddenly as a figure in a long tradition of individuals who abandoned what they perceived as the calcified pieties of their sects for what, in the particular denomination at hand, has been described by the theologian Karl Barth as "religionless Christianity." The very custom of which these figures availed themselves is built into itself, as it were. Protestantism, for example, protests. It preserves the right of the individual to reject institutional authority and does so because it views the freedom of the individual to contemplate her own humanity, her own self, as supremely sacred.

I have not strayed as far as it might seem. The work most alluded to throughout Shakespeare and Melville is the Bible. In *Moby-Dick*, the second most invoked works are those of Shakespeare. Melville, perceiving that holy darkness in Hawthorne's writing and then comparing Hawthorne to Shakespeare, completes a beautiful loop that embodies and avails itself of one of the deepest, first premises about faith in the Christian tradition, which is its failure. (Again, there is no necessity here to endorse Christianity in order to appreciate the beauty of the idea.) The failure of faith is practically synonymous with the failure of hope. The preservation of hope depends on each individual's freedom to search for it where she must, and the preservation of that freedom is sacrosanct.

Here, then, is another instance of the sort of sublime paradox across which Melville arrayed his prose; the hopeless man struggling against his hopelessness within the sanctuary of the very tradition in which he fears he does not or cannot believe. Art, like the best religion and philosophy, not only accepts paradox but thrives upon it, and it is this particular, ultimate, cosmic paradox that makes Melville's articles, novels, poems, and correspondence so electrifying. Any God, Truth, Idea, Beauty worth contemplating is certainly not required to satisfy or reduce to human rationality.

These letters embody and reproduce—reenact—both the process and results of this kind of thinking and composition. It is such a pleasure to watch Melville embark in each case with generous sentiments of domestic hospitality, with offers of a fire, a bed, a bottle of champagne or port (or brandy, or . . . !), and from there spiral out into his inevitable fathomless speculation. He is acutely aware of this phenomenon. It is involuntary. "What's the reason, Mr. Hawthorne, that in the last stages of metaphysics a fellow always falls to *swearing* so? I could rip an hour. You see, I began with a little criticism . . . and here I have landed in Africa." No sooner does he stop himself for a moment and declare, "But it's an endless sermon,—no more of it," than he plunges on with, "my old foible—preaching." That these letters do read much like homilies is a key to their power and genius.

Unlike the latest purveyors of re-treaded positivism, Melville was not interested in tenure or celebrity. He was not, to paraphrase Wittgenstein, a bourgeois philosopher, concerned with the consistency of his own theories rather than Truth with a capital "T." He writes to Hawthorne that "What I feel most moved to write, that is banned,—it will not pay. Yet altogether, write the *other* way I cannot," and that "Though I wrote the Gospels in this century I should die in the gutter." "Try to get a living by the Truth—and go to the Soup Societies." That old dark true self he found in Hawthorne's stories, that dark, brilliant self each and every one of us possesses, that persists and pursues and wakes us every night at the wolf hour with the very fact of itself—with the fact of ourselves *as* selves—despite every parlor trick we play to make it disappear or at least transmogrify from subject to predicate, as if it were all a matter of grammatical sleight of hand, holy if anything after all deserves the name—that is what he felt compelled to pursue in his own books, even at the cost of material prosperity. He refused to uncouple what Emerson called the "moral sweet" from the "material sweet." Every one of us since Adam and Eve has had one of those dark selves. What could be more democratic? What could be more worthy of Herman Melville's attention and his art, his veneration and his doubts? What could sound a deeper note and inspire greater recognition when he read and subsequently reached out—passionately and in fellowship—to Nathaniel Hawthorne?

Melville's writing is bracing in every instance. He reads so like a prophet because his milieu is after all exhortation, homiletics, his disposition that of a preacher in the pulpit, the pulpit being, as he tells Hawthorne in a letter, the very stronghold of Truth. That device of arraying the cosmos between opposites is a figure of speech continually used in Biblical literature, called *merism*, and it is always used inclusively—that is, good and evil, night and day, lord and servant, hope and despair are not opposed against one another but together comprehend an ontological whole larger than either alone. Either alone in fact is meaningless without the other against which to define it. And that inclusivity provides the very impulse for democratic sentiment, for putting the servant, the common sailor at the center of the whole cosmos, arranging the world between sailor and admiral, George Washington and a thief, God and servant. In the tradition, God stepped down into our human time, history, as a servant, a kind of ultimate merism itself. The transcendent God demonstrated His transcendence by becoming immanent, and the characterizing quality of His immanence was humility, self-effacement. The thrall in which this baffling and exhilarating idea held Melville is evident in every word he wrote and powers the novels, the poems, the letters. It is the same power that bursts the bounds of conventional decorous writing and gives way into the greatest realms of artistic inquiry—human inquiry—about ourselves in the universe, where not only can the tale be told by unlettered Ishmael, but Ishmael, made merely of ink as he is, can nevertheless possess all of the intellectual and poetic brilliance of his flesh and blood creator, Herman Melville, and by extension something like the thrilling, beautiful creative and narrative omniscience of the transcendent God who authored them both.

Paul Harding
Massachusetts

INTRODUCTION

by Mark Niemeyer

"Whence come you, Hawthorne? By what right do you drink from my flagon of life? And when I put it to my lips—lo, they are yours and not mine. I feel that the Godhead is broken up like the bread at the Supper, and that we are the pieces. Hence this infinite fraternity of feeling." It was in the middle of November 1851 when Herman Melville wrote these words expressing his joyful astonishment at the sense of brotherhood he felt towards his friend and fellow author Nathaniel Hawthorne, who had just sent him praise of the recently published *Moby-Dick*. Having by then known Hawthorne for more than a year, Melville could seemingly still not believe his good fortune in having met someone who appeared to him much more than a good friend—a man, Melville thought, who was his only real literary peer in the country, someone whose company he relished—a soul mate. But the closeness of that friendship was already almost over at that point. In fact, though the two writers had been living near each other in the Berkshires, in western Massachusetts, just a few days after Melville wrote those words, Hawthorne would move away. And if they remained friends for the rest of their lives, they would see each other again on only a few rare occasions—and the magic, one might say, was gone.

The two authors met for the first time on Monday, August 5, 1850 at a memorable gathering of literary personalities organized in the Berkshires by David Dudley Field, a resident of the area and himself the author of a local history. It was quite an event. Besides Melville and Hawthorne, the party included Oliver Wendell Holmes, the medical doctor who had already begun a parallel career as a writer; Hawthorne's publisher, James T. Fields, accompanied by his wife; Evert Duyckinck, a friend of Melville's and editor of the New York-based *Literary World*; Cornelius Mathews, an editor and writer who had accompanied Duyckinck (the two had been invited for a short vacation by Melville); and at least two local residents. In the morning the group climbed the picturesque Monument Mountain, and at midday Field hosted a dinner, during which a spirited and good-humored discussion of the relative merits of Englishmen and Americans helped enliven the conversation. Afterwards, joined by popular historian J. T. Headley, the group sallied out to explore the Icy Glen, another local curiosity.

On that day in 1850 Melville and Hawthorne saw each other for the first time, had the opportunity to hear each other speak about a variety of topics (though Melville probably did more talking than the generally reticent Hawthorne), and no doubt were able to squeeze in a least some short pieces of conversation between themselves. Both men were newcomers to the region. Hawthorne, at the end of May, had just moved with his wife Sophia and their two children, Julian and Una (their last child, Rose, would be born the next year), to a little red cottage in Lenox. Melville, who knew the area thanks to family connections, was there on vacation from New York City that August, though in September he would buy in nearby Pittsfield a farmhouse on 160 acres of land, which he named Arrowhead, and move there with his wife Elizabeth and son Malcolm (there would eventually be three more children: Stanwix, Elizabeth, and Frances), not to mention his mother and three of his sisters. And both men were at the peaks of their literary careers, though they may not have realized it at the time. Hawthorne had just published what is widely considered his masterpiece, *The Scarlet Letter*, in March, and was getting ready to begin work on *The House of the Seven Gables*, probably his second most highly esteemed work. Melville, for his part, was working on his own greatest achievement, *Moby-Dick*, which would be published the following year.

The two men clearly liked each other right away. Melville, in fact, was awestruck with the already famous Hawthorne, a kindred spirit, he clearly felt, who, at forty-six, was romantically handsome. And Hawthorne, too, was taken by Melville. The normally reserved New Englander, who had been born in Salem, Massachusetts, invited Melville, along with his guests from New York, to call on him two days after their first meeting. Hawthorne treated them to champagne, and the group walked out to the Stockbridge Bowl to take in the local scenery. More surprisingly, given his generally shy demeanor, Hawthorne asked Melville to spend a few days with him before he himself left the area. Clearly, there was a mutual attraction.

Melville's immediate reaction to Hawthorne is reflected in an essay he wrote just a few days after meeting him. "Hawthorne and His Mosses," written at the instigation of Evert Duyckinck—who took the essay with him when he returned to New York on Monday, August 12, and which he published in the August 17 and 24, 1850 issues of the *Literary World*—is ostensibly a review of Hawthorne's short story collection *Mosses from an Old Manse*, which had come out in 1846. But it's much more—and much less, one might argue—than that. In order to hide his identity, Melville published the essay under the byline of "A Virginian Spending July in Vermont." He was, of course, neither a Virginian (Melville had been born in New York City), nor spending July (or August, for that matter) in Vermont. The southern persona no doubt gave him a certain feeling of freedom, notably to use rhetorical flourishes—not to say occasional bombast—throughout the essay, especially in his praise of Hawthorne and his defense of American literature and American authors. And Melville's false claim at one point in the essay that he had never seen Hawthorne also helped conceal his identity.

"Hawthorne and His Mosses" begins by evoking a romantic pastoral scene, which helps put the unnamed reviewer in the mood for reading Hawthorne. The actual criticism of the individual stories (or tales, as they were generally called at the time) is sometimes a bit vague, but Melville offers extravagant praise for his fellow author. He notes the "blackness" in his writing, which, for Melville, "derives its force from its appeal to that Calvinistic sense of Innate Depravity and Original Sin." Furthermore, he declares, "it is that blackness in Hawthorne, of which I have spoken, that so fixes and fascinates me." Clearly caught up in his own enthusiasm, Melville then launches off on a discussion of William Shakespeare that leads, eventually, to an overt comparison between Hawthorne and the playwright who often serves as the ultimate touchstone of literary greatness in the English-speaking world. Melville knew that such a linking of the two names would seem exaggerated to some readers, but he tones down his enthusiasm only slightly in order to declare: "Now, I do not say that Nathaniel of Salem is a greater than William of Avon, or as great. But the difference between the two men is by no means immeasurable. Not a very great deal more, and Nathaniel were verily William." Hawthorne, Melville seemed convinced, was the greatest living American author—probably the greatest American author up to that point. At the same time, it should not be forgotten that Melville, as already mentioned, was working on *Moby-Dick*, which he must have known, on some level, would itself be a great book. His comment, for example, that "You must have plenty of sea-room to tell the Truth in" seems to be an allusion to that work. And when he states, "This, too, I mean, that if Shakespeare has not been equalled, he is sure to be surpassed, and surpassed by an American born now or yet to be born," he is no doubt speaking about himself as much as about Hawthorne.

Melville's essay also needs to be seen in the context of the mid-nineteenth-century American literary landscape, when the country's writers were still struggling to establish themselves and to prove that the United States could, in fact, create a literature good enough to rival that of Great Britain. The situation was made especially difficult by the absence throughout most of the century of an international copyright agreement between the United States and other countries, allowing, in many cases, large-scale pirating of literary works on both sides of the Atlantic. American writers, for their part, could not be sure that their works published in Great Britain would earn them any money (though in many cases fair-minded British publishers did pay their American authors), and, in the United States, they had to compete with popular British authors, like Dickens, whose works could be brought out by unscrupulous American publishers at low prices since there was no legal obligation to pay royalties. Besides supporting international copyright, American literary nationalists also tried to encourage writers in the United States to make use of themes that reflected distinctive aspects of the country. And they appealed to the patriotism of their fellow citizens, which Melville clearly does in his essay. "You must believe in Shakespeare's unapproachability, or quit the country," he writes. "But what sort of belief is this for an American, a man who is bound to carry republican progressiveness into Literature, as well as into Life? Believe me, my friends, that Shakespeares are this day being born on the banks of the Ohio. And the day will come, when you shall say who reads a book by an Englishman that is a modern?"[1] And Melville even advocates a sort of literary "affirmative action," to use an anachronism, stating: "let America first praise mediocrity even, in her own children, before she praises (for everywhere, merit demands acknowledgment from every one) the best excellence in the children of any other land. Let her own authors, I say, have the priority of appreciation." This type of rhetoric had been going on for decades by the time Melville penned "Hawthorne and His Mosses," and he was no doubt having a bit of fun playing with the exaggerated declarations of literary nationalists—which doesn't mean he didn't believe what he wrote.

A final dimension of "Hawthorne and His Mosses" that should be mentioned, especially in the context of the relationship between the two authors, is that parts of the essay read, in fact, like declarations of love. As already mentioned, Melville had been extraordinarily taken by Hawthorne when he had met him only a few days before, and these feelings come out quite clearly in a few passages of the essay. Near the beginning, Melville declares, "The soft ravishments of the man spun me round about in a web of dreams, and when the book was closed, when the spell was over, this wizard 'dismissed me with but misty reminiscences, as if I had been dreaming of him.'" The phrase "love and admiration" is used twice in the essay, and Melville's imagery gets highly suggestive when he writes, "But already I feel that this Hawthorne has dropped germinous seeds into my soul. He

---

1 In this passage, Melville offers a patriotic retort to Englishman Sydney Smith's gibe of thirty years before: "In the four quarters of the globe, who reads an American book?" (Review of *Statistical Annals of the United States of America*, by Adam Seybert, *The Edinburgh Review*, January 1820, 79).

expands and deepens down, the more I contemplate him; and further, and further, shoots his strong New-England roots into the hot soil of my Southern soul." To twenty-first century readers such passages appear obviously sexual, but it should be remarked that such an interpretation would have been less likely in the mid-nineteenth century. Certainly the religiously conservative Evert Duyckinck, who published the essay, saw no problem with them, but that there are strong sentiments being expressed is undeniable. Exactly how one should characterize them, however, is less certain.

If Melville expressed his "love and admiration" at first sight, so to speak, in "Hawthorne and His Mosses," the friendship between the two was confirmed soon after the publication of the essay when Melville spent several days in Lenox with Hawthorne and his family, staying with them from September 3 to 7. At some time during this period the Hawthornes learned that it was Melville who had written the review of *Mosses from an Old Manse*, a revelation that delighted both Nathaniel and Sophia. Over the course of the next sixteen months, the two authors, whose homes were about six miles apart, saw each other relatively often, though with each of them involved in intense writing and occupied with their families, not to mention being hampered at times by the Massachusetts winter, such opportunities were somewhat less frequent than they may have wished.

An eloquent testimony to the friendship between the two men is offered by the surviving letters that Melville wrote to Hawthorne, most of them dating from the period when the two were residing in the Berkshires. Unfortunately, Hawthorne's letters to Melville have been lost and may well have been destroyed by Melville (the single exception is a brief note dated March 27, 1851, in which Hawthorne asks for a few favors and thanks Melville for his hospitality during an overnight stay he had made accompanied by his daughter Una). Melville's letters, in a more informal and personal voice than that of "Hawthorne and His Mosses," demonstrate not just Melville's love and admiration for Hawthorne, but offer stunning examples of his powerful prose. They also make it clear that Hawthorne helped inspire Melville in his thoughts about literature and life, just as he was working on the composition of his masterpiece. Indeed, it is likely that the intellectual energy offered by the relationship helped shape *Moby-Dick*, perhaps, for example, in Melville's exploration of evil and his portrayal of Ahab as an obsessed tragic hero. To what extent Melville may have influenced the literary style of the older, more established Hawthorne is less clear, though it is possible that Melville's appreciation of Hawthorne's "blackness" led him to emphasize that element in his writings even more.

The ten extant letters were written in the relatively short span of time between January 1851, when the two authors had known each other for about six months, and December 1852. Some are relatively brief and matter-of-fact, like the first one, in which Melville invites Hawthorne and his family to come visit. Melville's second letter, written in April 1851, offers appreciative criticism of Hawthorne's recently published *The House of the Seven Gables*, an inscribed copy of which Hawthorne had given him as a gift. In this letter, Melville, declares, "There is the grand truth about Nathaniel Hawthorne. He says NO! in thunder; but the Devil himself cannot make him say *yes*. For all men who say *yes*, lie." The third letter was written the following month, when Melville was getting ready to go to New York to work on getting *Moby-Dick* ready for press. It reminds us that besides his writing, Melville also had to take care of various chores at Arrowhead.

Indeed, the comfortable, though somewhat old-fashioned, house, built in the late eighteenth century, needed frequent tending, as did the few farm animals and crops Melville had planted. And the letter makes it clear that one reason he appreciated his relationship with Hawthorne was that he could discuss ideas with his fellow author, ideas about concepts like truth, democracy, and fame. Melville also expresses in this letter his frustration at the fact that his working conditions were far from ideal. He complains to Hawthorne, "The calm, the coolness, the silent grass-growing mood in which a man *ought* always to compose,—that, I fear, can seldom be mine. Dollars damn me; and the malicious Devil is forever grinning in upon me, holding the door ajar."

The fourth letter was written in June 1851, after Melville's return from New York, with *Moby-Dick* still unfinished. Once again he speaks of the many tasks he had to contend with at Arrowhead and looks forward to seeing Hawthorne again so they can "talk ontological heroics together." And in this letter Melville reveals what he calls the secret motto of *Moby-Dick*. He only makes it partially explicit, citing the Latin phrase, "Ego non baptiso te in nomine" ("I do not baptize you in the name"), but whose full significance, suggesting that his book had plumbed the depths of evil, he apparently assumed Hawthorne would understand (see footnote n° 16, page 50). About a month later, Melville wrote a brief note to his neighbor, expressing his hope that they would see each other soon and dreaming that they would have time before the fall to "hit upon some little bit of vagabondism." If the "vagabondism" never took place, their visiting continued. On August 1, 1851, as a birthday present to himself, Melville rode over to see Hawthorne, and, with Hawthorne's wife Sophia—who normally forbade smoking in the sitting-room—not at home, the two talked late into the night. As Hawthorne wrote in his notebooks:

> After supper, I put Julian to bed; and Melville and I had a talk about time and eternity, things of this world and of the next, and books, and publishers, and all possible and impossible matters, that lasted pretty deep into the night; and if truth must be told, we smoked cigars even within the sacred precincts of the sitting-room. At last, he arose, and saddled his horse (whom we had put into the barn) and rode off for his own domicile; and I hastened to make the most of what little sleeping-time remained for me.[2]

Obviously, the two authors were on the best of terms and mutually appreciated their far-ranging intellectual discussions.

Well aware, of course, of his friend and neighbor's work-in-progress, Hawthorne offered a note of recognition of *Moby-Dick* near the end of his children's work, *A Wonder-Book*, published on November 8, 1851: "On the hither side of Pittsfield sits Herman Melville, shaping out the gigantic conception of his 'White Whale,' while the gigantic shape of Graylock looms upon him from his study-window." By the time this early allusion to the book was published, Melville's masterpiece had already come out in London under the title *The Whale.* Near the middle of November it was issued in New York as *Moby-Dick; or, The Whale.* Melville, for his part, made a more dramatic tribute to his fellow author in that work. Following the title page, was printed, "In Token of My Admiration for his Genius, This Book is Inscribed to Nathanial Hawthorne." It was most likely on November 14 that the two men met for a late midday dinner at the Little Red Inn in Lenox. There Melville presented an inscribed copy of the new book to Hawthorne, who, at some point during what must

---

2 Nathaniel Hawthorne, *The American Notebooks*, Ed. Claude M. Simpson (Columbus: Ohio State University Press, 1972), 448.

have been an enjoyable and moving afternoon, turned the title page to discover the book's dedication.

Just a few days later Hawthorne wrote a now lost "exultation-breeding letter," as Melville calls it, praising *Moby-Dick*, to which Melville responded on or near November 17. That letter is one of the most powerful of the group, and expresses ardently Melville's feelings of close brotherhood with Hawthorne. Melville was exuberant, in fact, at being appreciated and understood by the person whose literary opinion he valued most. And like some of the passages in "Hawthorne and His Mosses," certain phrases in this letter seem to express a genuine love, phrases such as the one quoted at the beginning of this introduction or another one, near the end of the letter, where the author declares, "I am content and can be happy. I shall leave the world, I feel, with more satisfaction for having come to know you. Knowing you persuades me more than the Bible of our immortality." And it is in this letter that Melville tells Hawthorne, "The divine magnet is in you, and my magnet responds." All of these heart-felt lines were written with the knowledge that Hawthorne would be leaving the Berkshires just a few days later, moving to West Newton, Massachusetts.

By the time Melville next wrote to Hawthorne, in July 1852, he had moved again, this time to Concord, Massachusetts. In a jovial voice, the letter offers congratulations to Hawthorne on his recently published work, *The Blithedale Romance*, an inscribed copy of which Hawthorne had sent to Melville. That the men were still on close terms is clear not only from the evidence of Melville's tone and Hawthorne's gift, but also in Melville's reference to an invitation from Hawthorne to come visit him in Concord, which Melville regretfully had to decline for the time being.

The last three letters, written in the second half of 1852, all concern the sad story of a woman named Agatha who married a shipwrecked sailor named Robertson. She was then abandoned by him for many years, Robertson entering into a bigamous marriage with another woman. He later returned after the death of this second wife, only to abandon Agatha again and marry a third woman. Melville had heard the story from a lawyer while visiting Nantucket. The type of long-suffering and patience it contained made him think it would be a perfect theme for Hawthorne, somewhat, perhaps, like that of *The Scarlet Letter.* In the first of the three letters, written in August, Melville gives a detailed description of the story as well as his thoughts for various literary touches that might be appropriate. He also enclosed a clerk's copy of an account of the story by the lawyer (included as an appendix in this volume) who had first told him about Agatha and who had been involved in legal proceedings related to Robertson's bigamy. In the second letter Melville offers a few more suggestions of how the story might be treated and expresses his hope of seeing Hawthorne again soon. In fact, Melville did visit Hawthorne in Concord on December 2, 1852, when, among other things, they discussed the story of Agatha face to face. Hawthorne apparently expressed doubts at that point about writing the story and suggested that Melville do it himself. And in Melville's last surviving letter to Hawthorne, written in the first half of December, he announced that he would, indeed, do so. Though the story was never published and though no manuscript survives, Melville apparently did, in fact, complete it under the title of *The Isle of the Cross.*[3]

---

3 See Hershel Parker, *Herman Melville: A Biography, Volume 2, 1851–1891* (Baltimore: Johns Hopkins U. P., 2002), chapter 7, "*The Isle of the Cross*: September 1852–June 1853," 136–161. Parker's two-volume biography is the most complete and most authoritative account of Melville's life and was an indispensable resource in the preparation of this introduction.

The next time the two men saw each other was in November 1856, when Melville, on an extended trip to Europe and the Holy Land, in part in an effort to improve his health, visited Hawthorne, who was serving as the United States consul in Liverpool and living in nearby Southport. They spent a week together, renewing their friendship and visiting the area, including an excursion to the town of Chester. By this time, Hawthorne's place as a major figure in American letters seemed secure, while Melville's own reputation, which had rarely been on a sure footing, seemed on the decline. Hawthorne's comments about Melville, recorded in his notebooks, offer a rare and poignant portrait of Melville at that time and merit being quoted from at length:

> *November 20th, Thursday.* A week ago last Monday, Herman Melville came to see me at the Consulate, looking much as he used to do (a little paler, and perhaps a little sadder), in a rough outside coat, and with his characteristic gravity and reserve of manner. . . . we soon found ourselves on pretty much our former terms of sociability and confidence. Melville has not been well, of late; he has been affected with neuralgic complaints in his head and limbs, and no doubt has suffered from too constant literary occupation, pursued without much success, latterly; and his writings, for a long while past, have indicated a morbid state of mind. . . .
>
> He stayed with us from Tuesday till Thursday; and, on the intervening day, we took a pretty long walk together, and sat down in a hollow among the sand hills (sheltering ourselves from the high, cool wind) and smoked a cigar. Melville, as he always does, began to reason of Providence and futurity, and of everything that lies beyond human ken, and informed me that he had 'pretty much made up his mind to be annihilated'; but still he does not seem to rest in that anticipation; and, I think, will never rest until he gets hold of a definite belief. It is strange how he persists—and

> has persisted ever since I knew him, and probably long before—in wandering to-and fro over these deserts, as dismal and monotonous as the sand hills amid which we were sitting. He can neither believe, nor be comfortable in his unbelief; and he is too honest and courageous not to try to do one or the other. If he were a religious man, he would be one of the most truly religious and reverential; he has a very high and noble nature, and better worth immortality than most of us.[4]

The relationship had changed, and so had the two men. Still friends, time had altered the circumstances of each. And by 1856, Melville and Hawthorne had both already published most of their major works, certainly most of the books that would eventually secure their popular and critical reputations. On the return leg of his trip, in May 1857, Melville stopped by the consulate in Liverpool to pick up a trunk he had left there and saw Hawthorne briefly once again. It would be their last meeting. Hawthorne, for his part, remained in Europe until 1860, when he moved back to Concord. In 1864 his health began to decline, and he died on May 19, while traveling with an old friend, former United States President Franklin Pierce. Melville, who had not seen Hawthorne for seven years, was "much shocked" according to his wife.[5]

If Hawthorne was gone, Melville had not forgotten him. As time went by, he reflected on the man who had meant so much to him, especially during that almost year and a half in 1850–1851

---

4 Nathaniel Hawthorne, *The English Notebooks, 1856–1860*, Ed. Thomas Woodson and Bill Ellis (Columbus: Ohio State University Press, 1997),162–163.

5 Hershel Parker, *Herman Melville: A Biography, Volume 2, 1851–1891* (Baltimore: Johns Hopkins U. P., 2002), 576.

in the Berkshires. Melville could no longer write to his friend, but he could write about him, and that's what, according to most critics, he did in his long poem *Clarel: A Poem and Pilgrimage in the Holy Land*, published in 1876. *Clarel* was inspired by Melville's trip to Palestine, which was part of the voyage during which he had met Hawthorne in Liverpool. It offers somewhat of a guided tour of Jerusalem and the surrounding area as well as considerations of philosophical questions of the day, including the status of various religious beliefs in the context of a modern culture less and less given to spirituality and faith. Clarel, the central character, is a young American theological student traveling in the Holy Land, himself doubtful of his faith. The aloof and mysterious character Vine—an aesthete whom Clarel finds intriguing and attractive—is widely believed to be based on Hawthorne, and in his portrayal of Vine, Melville seems to have dramatized his thoughts about his friend, whose literary reputation had been steadily climbing since his death.

The poem, however, is not simply a thinly veiled presentation of the relationship between Melville and Hawthorne, in part because the character who most resembles Melville is not, in fact, Clarel, but Rolfe, another member of the group of travelers, and in part because there are many other themes developed in the poem. In any case, the scene that most strongly seems to symbolically dramatize the early intellectual, emotional, and indeed, on some level, sexual attraction that Melville had had for Hawthorne appears in canto 27, "Vine and Clarel," of the second of the poem's four major parts, "The Wilderness." In that canto, Clarel is delighted when he spies Vine "through a leafy screen" and realizes they are alone together. The normally diffident Vine doesn't speak until "Clarel leaned—half laid— / Beside him." As Vine continues his discourse, Clarel's admiration, not to say desire, grows. He muses to himself about his "Prior advances unreturned" and fantasizes, thinking to himself, "O, now but for communion true / And close; let go each alien theme; / Give me thyself!" But Vine is either oblivious to Clarel's yearnings or willfully ignores them, and, in any case, his philosophizing goes on. When Vine pauses again, Clarel returns to his hopes for a genuine closeness, dreaming of "confidings that should wed / Our souls in one" and of Vine's calling him "*brother.*" And in this "passionate mood" Clarel lets fall some "inklings" of his feelings. Vine, however, once again ignores or is unaware of the sentiments Clarel tries to express. If in this passage Clarel and Vine do, in fact, represent Melville and Hawthorne, then it seems to confirm that at some point during that intense period in 1850–1851 Melville had had a strong admiration and love for Hawthorne, which was apparently not reciprocated in the way he had hoped.

The last piece of writing included in this collection is the short poem "Monody" (whose title means "an elegy or dirge performed by one person"). It was included in Melville's collection of poems *Timoleon Etc.*, published in 1891. There is disagreement as to whether this poem is, in fact, about Hawthorne. There is no absolute proof, but many people believe that it is a response by Melville to his friend's death in 1864, and the poem's theme does seem to invite such an interpretation. The poem speaks of knowing and loving a man and then becoming estranged from him, due to no fault on either side, only to have death seal the end of the relationship forever. And the reference to "the cloistral vine" in the next to last line seems to echo the name of the character Vine in *Clarel,* who, as previously noted, is also believed to be based on Hawthorne. Debate over whether or not the poem is about Hawthorne often focuses on the word "estranged." Some critics argue that after Hawthorne moved away from Lenox, or at least after Melville's visit to him in Concord in December 1852, a coolness, if not a sort of rupture occurred. Others argue that there is simply no evidence for such conjectures and that while the men did, indeed, grow apart after 1852, there was never any clear break in their friendship. These critics recall, for example, that when the two met in England in 1856, they quickly reestablished their "former terms of sociability and confidence," as Hawthorne had written in his notebooks. In any case, the theme and tone of the poem do seem to evoke what many people, at least, believe Melville's thoughts and feelings about Hawthorne at the time of his death (or sometime thereafter) may very well have been. And if that is, indeed, the case—despite the fact that the date of the poem's composition remains uncertain—the publication of "Monody" in 1891, the year of Melville's death, makes it, symbolically, his last word on the stimulating and passionate relationship he had had with the man he used to address as "My Dear Hawthorne."

Mark Niemeyer
Université de Bourgogne
Dijon, France

HERMAN MELVILLE'S LETTERS TO NATHANIEL HAWTHORNE

[29 JANUARY?] 1851

Pittsfield, Wednesday.

That side-blow thro' Mrs Hawthorne will not do.[6] I am not to be charmed out of my promised pleasure by any of that lady's syrenisms. *You*, Sir, I hold accountable, & the visit (in all its original integrity) must be made.—What! *spend the day*, only with us?—A Greenlander might as well talk of spending the day with a friend, when the day is only half an inch long.

As I said before, my best travelling chariot on runners, will be at your door, & provision made not only for the accommodation of all your family, but also for any quantity of *baggage*.

Fear not that you will cause the slightest trouble to us. Your bed is already made, & the wood marked for your fire. But a moment ago, I looked into the eyes of two fowls, whose tail feathers have been notched, as destined victims for the table. I keep the word "Welcome" all the time in my mouth, so as to be ready on the instant when you cross the threshold.

(By the way the old Romans you know had a *Salve*[7] carved in *their* thresholds)

Another thing, Mr Hawthorne—Do not think you are coming to any prim nonsensical house—that is

6 Mrs. Hawthorne's "side-blow" was apparently a promise that the Hawthornes would "spend the day" with the Melville family sometime soon. Melville was clearly hoping that they would come for more than just a day.

7 Latin; in this context meaning "welcome."

nonsensical in the ordinary way. You wont be much bored with punctilios. You may do what you please—say or say *not* what you please. And if you feel any inclination for that sort of thing—you may spend the period of your visit *in bed*, if you like—every hour of your visit.

Hark—There is some excellent Montado Sherry awaiting you & some most potent Port. We will have mulled wine with wisdom, & buttered toast with story-telling & crack jokes & bottles from morning till night.

Come—no nonsence. If you dont—I will send Constables after you.

On *Wednesday* then—weather & slieghing permitting I will be down for you about eleven o'clock A.M.

By the way—should Mrs Hawthorne for any reason conclude that *she*, for one, can not stay overnight with us—then *You* must—& the children, if you please.

H Melville

[16 APRIL?] 1851

Pittsfield, Wednesday morning.

My dear Hawthorne,—Concerning the young gentleman's shoes, I desire to say that a pair to fit him, of the desired pattern, cannot be had in all Pittsfield,—a fact which sadly impairs that metropolitan pride I formerly took in the capital of Berkshire.[8] Henceforth Pittsfield must hide its head. However, if a pair of bootees will at all answer, Pittsfield will be very happy to provide them. Pray mention all this to Mrs. Hawthorne, and command me.

"The House of the Seven Gables: A Romance. By Nathaniel Hawthorne. One vol. 16mo,[9] pp. 344."[10] The contents of this book do not belie its rich, clustering, romantic title. With great enjoyment we spent almost an hour in each separate gable. This book is like a fine old chamber, abundantly, but still judiciously, furnished with precisely that sort of furniture best fitted to furnish it. There are rich hangings, wherein are braided scenes from tragedies!

---

8 The Hawthornes had asked for Melville's help in finding a pair of shoes for their son Julian, born June 22, 1846.

9 Sextodecimo (or sixteenmo), indicating a book made from sheets of paper on either side of which sixteen pages were printed before being folded, sewn and cut. *The House of the Seven Gables*, however, was originally issued as an octavo (8vo), a book in which eight—rather than sixteen—leaves are made from each sheet. Melville may have been misled by the relatively small size of Hawthorne's romance for an octavo.

10 Hawthorne's *The House of the Seven Gables* was published on April 9, 1851. Hawthorne gave Melville an inscribed copy on April 11.

There is old china with rare devices, set out on the carved buffet; there are long and indolent lounges to throw yourself upon; there is an admirable sideboard, plentifully stored with good viands; there is a smell as of old wine in the pantry; and finally, in one corner, there is a dark little black-letter volume in golden clasps, entitled "Hawthorne: A Problem." It has delighted us; it has piqued a re-perusal; it has robbed us of a day, and made us a present of a whole year of thoughtfulness; it has bred great exhilaration and exultation with the remembrance that the architect of the Gables resides only six miles off, and not three thousand miles away, in England, say. We think the book, for pleasantness of running interest, surpasses the other works of the author. The curtains are more drawn; the sun comes in more; genialities peep out more. Were we to particularize what has most struck us in the deeper passages, we would point out the scene where Clifford, for a moment, would fain throw himself forth from the window to join the procession; or the scene where the Judge is left seated in his ancestral chair. Clifford is full of an awful truth throughout. He is conceived in the finest, truest spirit. He is no caricature. He is Clifford. And here we would say that, did circumstances permit, we should like nothing better than to devote an elaborate and careful paper to the full consideration and analysis of the purport and significance of what so strongly characterizes all of this author's writings. There is a certain tragic phase of humanity which, in our opinion, was never more powerfully embodied than by Hawthorne. We mean the tragicalness of human thought in its own unbiassed, native, and profounder workings. We think that into no recorded mind has the intense feeling of the visable truth ever entered more deeply than into this man's. By visable truth, we mean the apprehension of the absolute condition of present things as they strike the eye of the man who fears them not, though they do their worst to him,—the man who, like Russia or the British Empire, declares himself a sovereign nature (in himself) amid the powers of heaven, hell, and earth. He may perish; but so long as he exists he insists upon treating with all Powers upon an equal basis. If any of those other Powers choose to withhold certain secrets, let them; that does not impair my sovereignty in myself; that does not make me tributary. And perhaps, after all, there is *no* secret. We incline to think that the Problem of the Universe is like the Freemason's mighty secret, so terrible to all children. It turns out, at last, to consist in a triangle, a mallet, and an apron,—nothing more! We incline to think that God cannot explain His own secrets, and that He would like a little information upon certain points Himself. We mortals astonish Him as much as He us. But it is this *Being* of the matter; there lies the knot with which we choke ourselves. As soon as you say *Me*, a *God*, a *Nature*, so soon you jump off from your stool and hang from the beam. Yes, that word is the hangman. Take God out of the dictionary, and you would have Him in the street.

There is the grand truth about Nathaniel Hawthorne. He says NO! in thunder; but the Devil himself cannot make him say *yes*. For all men who say *yes*, lie; and all men who say *no*,—why, they are in the happy condition of judicious, unincumbered travellers in Europe; they cross the frontiers into Eternity with nothing but a carpet-bag,—that is to say, the Ego. Whereas those *yes*-gentry, they travel with heaps of baggage, and, damn them! they will never get through the Custom House. What's the reason, Mr. Hawthorne, that in the last stages of metaphysics a fellow always falls to *swearing* so? I could rip an hour. You see, I began with a little criticism extracted for your benefit from the "Pittsfield Secret Review," and here I have landed in Africa.

Walk down one of these mornings and see me. No nonsense; come. Remember me to Mrs. Hawthorne and the children.

H. Melville.

P.S. The marriage of Phoebe with the daguerreotypist is a fine stroke, because of his turning out to be a *Maule*. If you pass Hepzibah's cent-shop, buy me a Jim Crow (fresh) and send it to me by Ned Higgins.[11]

---

11 The names in the postscript are references to Hawthorne's *The House of the Seven Gables*, a gothic romance which takes place in the nineteenth century. One of the characters, Phoebe Pyncheon, marries Holgrave, the daguerreotypist. He is a descendant of Matthew Maule, who had been hanged for witchcraft by Colonel Pyncheon in the seventeenth century in order to gain possession of Maule's land, upon which he built the House of the Seven Gables. Hepzibah Pyncheon, an older unmarried woman, is Phoebe's cousin and lives in the house. Destitute, she opens a cent-shop on the ground floor in order to survive. Among the items for sale in the shop are gingerbread cookies in the shape of Jim Crow, a nineteenth-century racist caricature of blacks made famous by the song "Jump Jim Crow." Ned Higgins is a boy in the story who enjoys the Jim Crow gingerbreads.

[EARLY MAY] 1851[12]

My dear Hawthorne,—I should have been rumbling down to you in my pine-board chariot a long time ago, were it not that for some weeks past I have been more busy than you can well imagine,—out of doors,—building and patching and tinkering away in all directions. Besides, I had my crops to get in,—corn and potatoes (I hope to show you some famous ones by and by),—and many other things to attend to, all accumulating upon this one particular season. I work myself; and at night my bodily sensations are akin to those I have so often felt before, when a hired man, doing my day's work from sun to sun. But I mean to continue visiting you until you tell me that my visits are both supererogatory and superfluous. With no son of man do I stand upon any etiquette or ceremony, except the Christian ones of charity and honesty. I am told, my fellow-man, that there is an aristocracy of the brain. Some men have boldly advocated and asserted it. Schiller seems to have done so, though I don't know much about him. At any rate, it is true that there have been those who, while earnest in behalf of political equality, still accept the intellectual estates. And I can well perceive, I think, how a man of superior mind can, by its intense cultivation, bring himself, as it were, into a certain spontaneous aristocracy of feeling,—exceedingly nice and

12 The editors of the Northwestern-Newberry edition of Melville's *Correspondence* originally suggested "1 June?" 1851 as the date of this letter. Hershel Parker has redated it to "early May" 1851 (Hershel Parker, *Herman Melville: A Biography, Volume 1, 1819-1851* [Baltimore: Johns Hopkins U P, 1996], 841).

fastidious,—similar to that which, in an English Howard, conveys a torpedo-fish thrill at the slightest contact with a social plebeian. So, when you see or hear of my ruthless democracy on all sides, you may possibly feel a touch of a shrink, or something of that sort. It is but nature to be shy of a mortal who boldly declares that a thief in jail is as honorable a personage as Gen. George Washington. This is ludicrous. But Truth is the silliest thing under the sun. Try to get a living by the Truth—and go to the Soup Societies. Heavens! Let any clergyman try to preach the Truth from its very stronghold, the pulpit, and they would ride him out of his church on his own pulpit bannister. It can hardly be doubted that all Reformers are bottomed upon the truth, more or less; and to the world at large are not reformers almost universally laughing-stocks? Why so? Truth is ridiculous to men. Thus easily in my room here do I, conceited and garrulous, reverse the test of my Lord Shaftesbury.[13]

It seems an inconsistency to assert unconditional democracy in all things, and yet confess a dislike to all mankind—in the mass. But not so.—But it's an endless sermon,—no more of it. I began by saying that the reason I have not been to Lenox is this,—in the evening I feel completely done up, as the phrase is, and incapable of the long jolting to get to your house and back. In a week or so, I go to New York, to bury myself in a third-story room, and work and slave on my "Whale" while it is driving through the press.[14] *That* is the only way I can finish it now,—I am so pulled hither and thither by circumstances. The calm, the coolness, the silent grass-growing mood in which a

13 Anthony Ashley Cooper, Third Earl of Shaftesbury (1671-1713) was an English politician and philosopher. In "An Essay on the Freedom of Wit and Humor," included in *Characteristicks of Men, Manners, Opinions, Times* (first published in 1711), he asserts that the test of truth is its ability to bear ridicule. Here, Melville "reverses" Shaftesbury in claiming that truth is almost invariably perceived in the world as ridiculous.

14 Melville's most famous book was published under the title *The Whale* in London in October 1851 and under the title *Moby-Dick; or, The Whale* in November 1851.

man *ought* always to compose,—that, I fear, can seldom be mine. Dollars damn me; and the malicious Devil is forever grinning in upon me, holding the door ajar. My dear Sir, a presentiment is on me,—I shall at last be worn out and perish, like an old nutmeg-grater, grated to pieces by the constant attrition of the wood, that is, the nutmeg. What I feel most moved to write, that is banned,—it will not pay. Yet, altogether, write the *other* way I cannot. So the product is a final hash, and all my books are botches. I'm rather sore, perhaps, in this letter; but see my hand!—four blisters on this palm, made by hoes and hammers within the last few days. It is a rainy morning; so I am indoors, and all work suspended. I feel cheerfully disposed, and therefore I write a little bluely. Would the Gin were here! If ever, my dear Hawthorne, in the eternal times that are to come, you and I shall sit down in Paradise, in some little shady corner by ourselves; and if we shall by any means be able to smuggle a basket of champagne there (I won't believe in a Temperance Heaven), and if we shall then cross our celestial legs in the celestial grass that is forever tropical, and strike our glasses and our heads together, till both musically ring in concert,—then, O my dear fellow-mortal, how shall we pleasantly discourse of all the things manifold which now so distress us,—when all the earth shall be but a reminiscence, yea, its final dissolution an antiquity. Then shall songs be composed as when wars are over; humorous, comic songs,—"Oh, when I lived in that queer little hole called the world," or, "Oh, when I toiled and sweated below," or, "Oh, when I knocked and was knocked in the fight"—yes, let us look forward to such things. Let us swear that, though now we sweat, yet it is because of the dry heat which is indispensable to the nourishment of the vine which is to bear the grapes that are to give us the champagne hereafter.

But I was talking about the "Whale." As the fishermen say, "he's in his flurry" when I left him some three weeks ago. I'm going to take him by his jaw, however, before long, and finish him up in some fashion or other. What's the use of elaborating what, in its very essence, is so short-lived as a modern book? Though I wrote the Gospels in this century, I should die in the gutter.—I talk all about myself, and this is selfishness and egotism. Granted. But how help it? I am writing to you; I know little about you, but something about myself. So I write about myself,—at least, to you. Don't trouble yourself, though, about writing; and don't trouble yourself about visiting; and when you *do* visit, don't trouble yourself about talking. I will do all the writing and visiting and talking myself.—By the way, in the last "Dollar Magazine" I read "The Unpardonable Sin." He was a sad fellow, that Ethan Brand. I have no doubt you are by this time responsible for many a shake and tremor of the tribe of "general readers." It is a frightful poetical creed that the cultivation of the brain eats out the heart. But it's my *prose* opinion that in most cases, in those men who have fine brains and work them well, the heart extends down to hams. And though you smoke them with the fire of tribulation, yet, like veritable hams, the head only gives the richer and the better flavor. I stand for the heart. To the dogs with the head! I had rather be a fool with a heart, than Jupiter Olympus with his head. The reason the mass of men fear God, and *at bottom dislike* Him, is because they rather distrust His heart, and fancy Him all brain like a watch. (You perceive I employ a capital initial in the pronoun referring to the Deity; don't you think there is a slight dash of flunkeyism in that usage?) Another thing. I was in New York for four-and-twenty hours the other day, and saw a portrait of N. H. And I have seen and heard many flattering (in a publisher's point of view) allusions to the "Seven Gables." And I have seen "Tales," and "A New Volume" announced, by N. H. So upon the whole, I say to myself, this N. H. is in the ascendant. My dear Sir, they begin to patronize. All Fame is patronage. Let me be infamous: there is no patronage in *that*. What "reputation" H. M. has is horrible. Think of it! To go down to posterity is bad enough, any way; but to go down as a "man who lived among the cannibals"! When I speak of posterity, in reference to myself, I only mean the babies who will probably be born in the moment immediately ensuing upon my giving up the ghost. I shall go down to some of them, in all likelihood. "Typee" will be given to them, perhaps, with their gingerbread.[15] I have come to regard this matter of Fame as the most transparent of all vanities. I read Solomon more and more, and every time see deeper and deeper and unspeakable meanings in him. I did not think of Fame, a year ago, as I do now. My development has been all within a few years past. I am like one of those seeds taken out of the Egyptian Pyramids, which, after being three thousand years a seed and nothing but a seed, being planted in English soil, it developed itself, grew to greenness, and then fell to mould. So I. Until I was twenty-five, I had no development at all. From my twenty-fifth year I date my life. Three weeks have scarcely passed, at any time between then and now, that I have not unfolded within myself. But I feel that I am now come to the inmost leaf of the bulb, and that shortly the flower must fall to the mould. It seems to me now that Solomon was the truest man who ever spoke, and yet that he a little *managed* the truth with a view to popular conservatism; or else there have been many corruptions and interpolations of the text—In reading some of Goethe's sayings, so worshipped by his votaries, I came across this, *"Live in the all."* That is to say, your separate identity is but a wretched one,—good; but get out of yourself, spread and expand yourself, and bring to yourself the tinglings of life that are felt in the flowers and the woods, that are felt in the planets Saturn and Venus, and the Fixed Stars. What nonsense! Here is a fellow with a raging toothache. "My dear boy," Goethe says to him, "you are sorely afflicted with that tooth; but you must *live in the all,* and then you

15 Melville's first book, *Typee: A Peep at Polynesian Life*, was published in 1846.

will be happy!" As with all great genius, there is an immense deal of flummery in Goethe, and in proportion to my own contact with him, a monstrous deal of it in me.

H. Melville.

P.S. "Amen!" saith Hawthorne.

N.B. This "all" feeling, though, there is some truth in. You must often have felt it, lying on the grass on a warm summer's day. Your legs seem to send out shoots into the earth. Your hair feels like leaves upon your head. This is the *all* feeling. But what plays the mischief with the truth is that men will insist upon the universal application of a temporary feeling or opinion.

P.S. You must not fail to admire my discretion in paying the postage on this letter.

29 JUNE 1851

Pittsfield—June 29th

My dear Hawthorne—The clear air and open window invite me to write to you. For some time past I have been so busy with a thousand things that I have almost forgotten when I wrote you last, and whether I received an answer. This most persuasive season has now for weeks recalled me from certain crotchetty and over doleful chimaeras, the like of which men like you and me and some others, forming a chain of God's posts round the world, must be content to encounter now and then, and fight them the best way we can. But come they will,—for, in the boundless, trackless, but still glorious wild wilderness through which these outposts run, the Indians do sorely abound, as well as the insignificant but still stinging mosquitoes. Since you have been here, I have been building some shanties of houses (connected with the old one) and likewise some shanties of chapters and essays. I have been plowing and sowing and raising and painting and printing and praying,—and now begin to come out upon a less bustling time, and to enjoy the calm prospect of things from a fair piazza at the north of the old farm house here.

Not entirely yet, though, am I without something to be urgent with. The "Whale" is only half through the press; for, wearied with the long delay of the printers, and disgusted with the heat and dust of the babylonish brick-kiln of New York, I came back to the country to feel the grass—and end the book reclining on it, if I may.—I am sure you will pardon this speaking all about myself,—for if I *say* so much on that head, be sure all the rest of the world are thinking about themselves ten times as much. Let us speak, though we show all our faults and weaknesses,—for it is a sign of strength to be weak, to know it, and out with it,—not in set way and ostentatiously, though, but incidentally and without premeditation.—But I am falling into my old foible—preaching. I am busy, but shall not be very long. Come and spend a day here, if you can and want to; if not, stay in Lenox, and God give you long life. When I am quite free of my present engagements, I am going to treat myself to a ride and a visit to you. Have ready a bottle of brandy, because I always feel like drinking that heroic drink when we talk ontological heroics together. This is rather a crazy letter in some respects, I apprehend. If so, ascribe it to the intoxicating effects of the latter end of June operating upon a very susceptible and peradventure febrile temperament.

Shall I send you a fin of the *Whale* by way of a specimen mouthful? The tail is not yet cooked—though the hell-fire in which the whole book is broiled might not unreasonably have cooked it all ere this. This is the book's motto (the secret one),—Ego non baptiso te in nomine—but make out the rest yourself.[16]

H. M.

---

16 The Latin "motto" reads "I do not baptize you in the name. . . ." As Hershel Parker points out, "Melville was recalling Francis Palgrave's essay on 'Superstition and Knowledge,' which he had read in the July 1823 issue of the *Quarterly Review* or elsewhere" (*Herman Melville: A Biography, Volume 1, 1819-1851* [Baltimore: Johns Hopkins University Press, 1996], 847). The complete phrase, supposedly used by crazed witch-hunters, was *Ego non baptize te in nomine Patris et Filii et Spiritus Sancti—sed in nomine Diaboli* (I do not baptize you in the name of the Father and the Son and Holy Spirit—but in the name of the Devil). As Parker also points out, "In echoing to Hawthorne this witch-hunter's formula, Melville was anticipating that reviewers might respond to his prophetic truth-telling by treating him once again as a devilish opponent of Christianity. Any of his dark passages, however splendid, might be seized upon by witch-hunting reviewers who, from the time the man of the *Evangelist* rose up against him in 1846 [in a review of Melville's first book, *Typee*], had sought to drive him from authorship" (Parker, 847). In *Moby-Dick*, as he baptizes with blood the harpoon he hopes will kill the white whale, Ahab howls, "Ego non baptizo te in nomine patris, sed in nomine diaboli!" (chapter 113, "The Forge").

22 JULY 1851

Tuesday afternoon.

My dear Hawthorne:

This is not a letter, or even a note—but only a passing word said to you over your garden gate. I thank you for your easy-flowing long letter (received yesterday) which flowed through me, and refreshed all my meadows, as the Housatonic—opposite me—does in reality. I am now busy with various things—not incessantly though; but enough to require my frequent tinkerings; and this is the height of the haying season, and my nag is dragging me home his winter's dinners all the time. And so, one way and another, I am not yet a disengaged man; but shall be, very soon. Meantime, the earliest good chance I get, I shall roll down to you.

My dear fellow-being, we—that is, you and I—must hit upon some little bit of vagabondism, before Autumn comes. Graylock—we must go and vagabondize there. But ere we start we must dig a deep hole and bury all Blue Devils, there to abide till the Last Day. . . .

Goodbye,
his X mark.

[17?] NOVEMBER 1851

Pittsfield, Monday afternoon.

My dear Hawthorne: People think that if a man has undergone any hardship, he should have a reward; but for my part, if I have done the hardest possible day's work, and then come to sit down in a corner and eat my supper comfortably—why, then I don't think I deserve any reward for my hard day's work—for am I not now at peace? Is not my supper good? My peace and my supper are my reward, my dear Hawthorne. So your joy-giving and exultation-breeding letter[17] is not my reward for my ditcher's work with that book, but is the good goddess's bonus over and above what was stipulated for—for not one man in five cycles, who is wise, will expect appreciative recognition from his fellows, or any one of them. Appreciation! Recognition! Is Jove appreciated? Why, ever since Adam, who has got to the meaning of his great allegory—the world? Then we pigmies must be content to have our paper allegories but ill comprehended. I say your appreciation is my glorious gratuity. In my proud, humble way,—a shepherd-king,—I was lord of a little vale in the solitary Crimea; but you have now given me the crown of India. But on trying it on my head, I found it fell down on my ears, notwithstanding their asinine length—for it's only such ears that sustain such crowns.

Your letter was handed me last night on the road going to Mr. Morewood's, and I read it there. Had I been at home, I

17 Hawthorne had written an appreciative letter to Melville about *Moby-Dick*, which had just been published. The letter remains unlocated.

would have sat down at once and answered it. In me divine magnanimities are spontaneous and instantaneous—catch them while you can. The world goes round, and the other side comes up. So now I can't write what I felt. But I felt pantheistic then—your heart beat in my ribs and mine in yours, and both in God's. A sense of unspeakable security is in me this moment, on account of your having understood the book. I have written a wicked book, and feel spotless as the lamb. Ineffable socialities are in me. I would sit down and dine with you and all the gods in old Rome's Pantheon. It is a strange feeling—no hopefulness is in it, no despair. Content—that is it; and irresponsibility; but without licentious inclination. I speak now of my profoundest sense of being, not of an incidental feeling.

Whence come you, Hawthorne? By what right do you drink from my flagon of life? And when I put it to my lips—lo, they are yours and not mine. I feel that the Godhead is broken up like the bread at the Supper, and that we are the pieces. Hence this infinite fraternity of feeling. Now, sympathizing with the paper, my angel turns over another page. You did not care a penny for the book. But, now and then as you read, you understood the pervading thought that impelled the book—and that you praised. Was it not so? You were archangel enough to despise the imperfect body, and embrace the soul. Once you hugged the ugly Socrates because you saw the flame in the mouth, and heard the rushing of the demon,—the familiar,—and recognized the sound; for you have heard it in your own solitudes.

My dear Hawthorne, the atmospheric skepticisms steal into me now, and make me doubtful of my sanity in writing you thus. But, believe me, I am not mad, most noble Festus![18]

---

18 Porcius Festus was procurator of Judea from about 60 to 62 A.D. When the Apostle Paul was brought before him on various charges, Festus declared that he spoke like a madman: "And as he thus spake for himself, Festus said with a loud voice, Paul, thou art beside thyself; much learning doth make thee mad. But he said, I am not mad, most noble Festus; but speak forth the words of truth and soberness" (Acts 26.24-25 [King James Version]). With this allusion, Melville defends the exuberant, if not incoherent, tone and style of his letter.

But truth is ever incoherent, and when the big hearts strike together, the concussion is a little stunning. Farewell. Don't write a word about the book. That would be robbing me of my miserly delight. I am heartily sorry I ever wrote anything about you—it was paltry. Lord, when shall we be done growing? As long as we have anything more to do, we have done nothing. So, now, let us add Moby Dick to our blessing, and step from that. Leviathan is not the biggest fish;—I have heard of Krakens.

This is a long letter, but you are not at all bound to answer it. Possibly, if you do answer it, and direct it to Herman Melville, you will missend it—for the very fingers that now guide this pen are not precisely the same that just took it up and put it on this paper. Lord, when shall we be done changing? Ah! it's a long stage, and no inn in sight, and night coming, and the body cold. But with you for a passenger, I am content and can be happy. I shall leave the world, I feel, with more satisfaction for having come to know you. Knowing you persuades me more than the Bible of our immortality.

What a pity, that, for your plain, bluff letter, you should get such gibberish! Mention me to Mrs. Hawthorne and to the children, and so, good-by to you, with my blessing.

Herman.

I can't stop yet. If the world was entirely made up of Magians,[19] I'll tell you what I should do. I should have a paper-mill established at one end of the house, and so have an endless riband of foolscap[20] rolling in upon my desk; and upon that endless riband I should write a thousand—a million—billion thoughts, all under the form of a letter to you. The divine magnet is in you, and my magnet responds.

---

19 Magicians or sorcerers.

20 Paper. Foolscap was formerly a standard paper size in Great Britain, so called because it contained a watermark with the image of the head of a fool or jester wearing a cap and bells.

Which is the biggest? A foolish question—they are *One.*

H.

Don't think that by writing me a letter, you shall always be bored with an immediate reply to it—and so keep both of us delving over a writing-desk eternally. No such thing! I sha'n't always answer your letters, and you may do just as you please.

17 JULY 1852

By the way, here's a crown. Significant this. Pray, allow me to place it on your head in victorious token of your "Blithedale" success. Tho' not in strict keeping, I have embellished it with a plume.[21]

Pittsfield, July 17th

My Dear Hawthorne:—This name of "*Hawthorne*" seems to be ubiquitous. I have been on something of a tour lately, and it has saluted me vocally & typographically in all sorts of places & in all sorts of ways.—I was at the solitary Crusoeish island of Naushon (one of the Elizabeth group) and there, on a stately piazza, I saw it gilded on the back of a very new book, and in the hands of a clergyman.—I went to visit a gentleman in Brooklyne, and as we were sitting at our wine, in came the lady of the house, holding a beaming volume in her hand, from the city—"My Dear," to her husband, "I have brought you *Hawthorne's* new book." I entered the cars at Boston for this place. In came a lively boy "*Hawthorne's* new book!"—In good time I arrived home. Said my lady-wife "there is Mr *Hawthorne's* new book, come by mail" And this morning, lo! on my table a little note, subscribed *Hawthorne* again.—Well, the Hawthorne is a sweet flower; may it flourish in every hedge.

---

21 This light-hearted note offers congratulations to Hawthorne on his recent publication of *The Blithedale Romance*, a copy of which Hawthorne had his publisher send to Melville. The note makes reference to the paper manufacturer's embossed crown, to which Melville had affixed a small "plume."

I am sorry, but I can not at present come to see you at Concord as you propose.—I am but just returned from a two weeks' absence; and for the last three months & more I have been an utter idler and a savage—out of doors all the time. So, the hour has come for me to sit down again.

Do send me a specimen of your sand-hill, and a sunbeam from the countenance of Mrs: Hawthorne, and a vine from the curly arbor of Master Julian.

As I am only just home, I have not yet got far into the book but enough to see that you have most admirably employed materials which are richer than I had fancied them. Especially at this day, the volume is welcome, as an antidote to the mooniness of some dreamers—who are merely dreamers——Yet who the devel aint a dreamer?

H Melville

My rememberances to Miss Una & Master Julian—& the "compliments" & perfumes of the season to the "Rose-Bud."[22]

22 Reference to Hawthorne's third child, Rose, born on May 20, 1851.

13 AUGUST 1852[23]

Pittsfield Aug: 13th 1852.

While visiting Nantucket some four weeks ago, I made the acquaintance of a gentleman from New Bedford, a lawyer, who gave me considerable information upon several matters concerning which I was curious.—One night we were talking, I think, of the great patience, & endurance, & resignedness of the women of the island in submitting so uncomplainingly to the long, long abscences of their sailor husbands, when, by way of anecdote, this lawyer gave me a leaf from his professional experience. Altho' his memory was a little confused with regard to some of the items of the story, yet he told me enough to awaken the most lively interest in me; and I begged him to be sure and send me a more full account so soon as he arrived home—he having previously told me that at the time of the affair he had made a record in his books.—I heard nothing more, till a few days after arriving here at Pittsfield I received thro' the Post Office the enclosed document.—You will perceive by the gentleman's note to me that he assumed that I purposed making literary use of the story; but I had not hinted anything of the kind to him, & my first spontaneous interest in it arose from very different considerations.[24] I confess,

---

23 This letter details the unusual story of a woman named Agatha who married a shipwrecked sailor, who abandoned her for seventeen years, only to return and then abandon her again.

24 John H. Clifford's letter, which Melville included with this letter to Hawthorne, has been lost. A clerk's transcription of Clifford's account of Agatha's story, which Melville included in his letter to Hawthorne, however, is preserved in the Melville Collection of the Houghton Library at Harvard University. The transcription, which includes a postscript by Clifford himself, is reproduced in an appendix to this book.

however, that since then I have a little turned the subject over in my mind with a view to a regular story to be founded on these striking incidents. But, thinking again, it has occurred to me that this thing lies very much in a vein, with which you are peculiarly familiar. To be plump, I think that in this matter you would make a better hand at it than I would.—Besides the thing seems naturally to gravitate towards you (to speak . . . should of right belong to you. I could . . . the Steward to deliver it to you.—

The very great interest I felt in this story while narrating to me, was heightened by the emotion of the gentleman who told it, who evinced the most unaffected sympathy in it, tho' now a matter of his past.—But perhaps this great interest of mine may have been largely helped by some accidental circumstances or other; so that, possibly, to you the story may not seem to possess so much of pathos, & so much of depth. But you will see how it is.——

In estimating the character of Robinson charity should be allowed a liberal play. I take exception to that passage from the Diary which says that "*he must have received a portion of his punishment in this life*"—thus hinting of a future supplemental castigation.—I do not at all suppose that his desertion of his wife was a premeditated thing. If it had been so, he would have changed his name, probably, after quitting her.—No: he was a weak man, & his temptations (tho' we know little of them) were strong. The whole sin stole upon him insensibly—so that it would perhaps have been hard for him to settle upon the exact day when he could say to himself, "*Now* I have deserted my wife; unless, indeed upon the day he wedded the Alexandran lady.—And here I am reminded of your *London husband*; tho' the cases so widely contrast.[25]—Many more things might be mentioned; but I

25 The "*London husband*" appears in Hawthorne's "Wakefield," first published in 1835 and collected in *Twice-Told Tales* (1837; enlarged edition, 1842). The character Wakefield also abandons his wife.

forbear; you will find out the suggestiveness for yourself; & all the better perhaps, for my not intermeddling.———

If you should be sufficiently interested, to engage upon a regular story founded on this narration; then I consider you but fairly entitled to the following tributary items, collected by me, by chance, during my strolls thro the islands; & which—as you will perceive—seem legitimately to belong to the story, in its rounded & beautified & thoroughly developed state;—but of all this you must of course be your own judge—I but submit matter to you—I dont decide.

Supposing the story to open with the wreck—then there must be a storm; & it were well if some faint shadow of the preceding *calm* were thrown forth to lead the whole.—Now imagine a high cliff overhanging the sea & crowned with a pasture for sheep; a little way off—higher up,—a light-house, where resides the father of the future Mrs Robinson the First. The afternoon is mild & warm. The sea with an air of solemn deliberation, with an elaborate deliberation, ceremoniously rolls upon the beach. The air is suppressedly charged with the sound of long lines of surf. There is no land over against this cliff short of Europe & the West Indies. Young Agatha (but you must give her some other name) comes wandering along the cliff. She marks how the continual assaults of the sea have undermined it; so that the fences fall over, & have need of many shiftings inland. The sea has encroached also upon that part where their dwelling-house stands near the light-house.—Filled with meditations, she reclines along the edge of the cliff & gazes out seaward. She marks a handful of cloud on the horizon, presaging a storm thro' all this quietude. (Of a maratime family & always dwelling on the coast, she is learned in these matters) This again gives food for thought. Suddenly she catches the long shadow of the cliff cast upon the beach 100 feet beneath her; and now she notes a shadow moving along the shadow. It is cast by a sheep from the pasture. It has advanced to the very edge of the cliff, & is sending a mild innocent glance far out upon the water. There, in strange & beautiful contrast, we have the innocence of the land placidly eyeing the malignity of the sea. (All this having poetic reference to Agatha & her sea-lover, who is coming in the storm: the storm carries her lover to her; she catches a dim distant glimpse of his ship ere quitting the cliff.)——P.S. It were well, if from her knowledge of the deep miseries produced to wives by marrying seafaring men, Agatha should have formed a young determination never to marry a sailor; which resolve in her, however, is afterwards overborne by the omnipotence of Love.—P.S. No 2. Agatha should be active during the wreck, & should, in some way, be made the saviour of young Robinson. He should be the only survivor. He should be ministered to by Agatha at the house during the illness ensuing upon his injuries from the wreck.—Now this wrecked ship has driven over the shoals, & driven upon the beach where she goes to peices, all but her stem-part. This in course of time becomes embedded in the sand—after the lapse of some years showing nothing but the sturdy stem (or, prow-bone) projecting some two feet at low water. All the rest is filled & packed down with the sand.—So that after her husband has disappeared the sad Agatha every day sees this melancholy monument, with all its remindings.————

After a sufficient lapse of time—when Agatha has become alarmed about the protracted abscence of her young husband & is feverishly expecting a letter from him—then we must introduce the mail-post—no, that phrase wont' do, but here is the *thing.*—Owing to the remoteness of the lighthouse from any settled place no regular mail reaches it. But some mile or so distant there is a road leading between two post-towns. And at the junction of what we shall call the Light-House road with this Post Rode, there stands a post surmounted with a little rude wood box with a lid to it & a leather hinge. Into this box the Post boy drops all letters for the people of the light house & that vicinity of fishermen. To this *post* they must come for their letters. And, of course, daily young Agatha goes—for seventeen years she goes thither daily As her hopes gradually decay in her, so does the post itself & the little box decay. The post rots in the ground at last. Owing to its being little used—hardly used at all—grass grows rankly about it. At last a little bird nests in it. At last the post falls.

The father of Agatha must be an old widower—a man of the sea, but early driven away from it by repeated disasters. Hence, is he subdued & quiet & wise in his life. And now he tends a light house, to warn people from those very perils, from which he himself has suffered.

Some few other items occur to me—but nothing material—and I fear to weary you, if not, make you smile at my strange impertinent officiousness.—And it would be so, were it not that these things do, in my mind, seem legitimately to belong to the story; for they were visably suggested to me by scenes I actually beheld while on the very coast where the story of Agatha occurred.—I do not therefore, My Dear Hawthorne, at all imagine that you will think that I am so silly as to flatter myself I am giving you anything of my own. I am but restoring to you your own property—which you would quickly enough have identified for yourself—had you but been on the spot as I happened to be.

Let me conclude by saying that it seems to me that with your great power in these things, you can construct a story of remarkable interest out of this material furnished by the New Bedford lawyer.—You have a skeleton of actual reality to build about with fulness & veins & beauty. And if I thought I could do it as well as you, why, I should not let you have it.—The narrative from the Diary is instinct with significance.—Consider the mention of the *shawls*—& the inference derived from it. Ponder the conduct of this Robinson throughout.—Mark his trepidation & suspicion when any one called upon him.—But why prate so—you will mark it all & mark it deeper than I would, perhaps.

I have written all this in a great hurry; so you must spell it out the best way you may.

25 OCTOBER 1852

Monday Morning
25th Oct: 1852.

My Dear Hawthorne—

If you thought it worth while to write the story of Agatha, and should you be engaged upon it; then I have a little idea touching it, which however trifling, may not be entirely out of place. Perhaps, tho', the idea has occurred to yourself.—The probable facility with which Robinson first leaves his wife & then takes another, may, possibly, be ascribed to the peculiarly latitudinarian notions, which most sailors have of all tender obligations of that sort. In his previous sailor life Robinson had found a wife (for a night) in every port. The sense of the obligation of the marriage-vow to Agatha had little weight with him at first. *It* was only when some years of life ashore had passed that his moral sense on that point became develloped. And hence his subsequent conduct—Remorse &c. Turn this over in your mind & see if it is right. If not—make it so yourself.

If you come across a little book called "Taughconic"—look into it and divert yourself with it. Among others, you figure in it, & I also. But you are the most honored, being the most abused, and having the greatest space allotted you.—It is a "Guide Book" to Berkshire.

I dont know when I shall see you. I shall lay eyes on you one of these days however. Keep some Champagne or Gin for me.

My respects and best remembrances to Mrs: Hawthorne & a reminder to the children.

H Melville

If you find any *sand* in this letter, regard it as so many sands of my life, which run out as I was writing it.

BETWEEN 3 AND 13 DECEMBER 1852

Boston.

My dear Hawthorne,—The other day, at Concord, you expressed uncertainty concerning your undertaking the story of Agatha, and, in the end, you urged *me* to write it. I have decided to do so, and shall begin it immediately upon reaching home; and so far as in me lies, I shall endeavor to do justice to so interesting a story of reality. Will you therefore enclose the whole affair to me; and if anything of your own has occurred to you in your random thinking, won't you note it down for me on the same page with my memorandum? I wish I had come to this determination at Concord, for then we might have more fully and closely talked over the story, and so struck out new light. Make amends for this, though, as much as you conveniently can. With your permission I shall make use of the "Isle of Shoals," as far as the name goes at least. I shall also introduce the old Nantucket seaman, in the way I spoke to you about. I invoke your blessing upon my endeavors; and breathe a fair wind upon me. I greatly enjoyed my visit to you, and hope that you reaped some corresponding pleasure.

H. Melville.

Julian, Una, and Rose,—my salutations to them.

HAWTHORNE AND HIS MOSSES[26]

By a Virginian Spending July in Vermont

A PAPERED chamber in a fine old farm-house—a mile from any other dwelling, and dipped to the eaves in foliage—surrounded by mountains, old woods, and Indian ponds,—this, surely, is the place to write of Hawthorne. Some charm is in this northern air, for love and duty seem both impelling to the task. A man of a deep and noble nature has seized me in this seclusion. His wild, witch voice rings through me; or, in softer cadences, I seem to hear it in the songs of the hill-side birds, that sing in the larch trees at my window.

Would that all excellent books were foundlings, without father or mother, that so it might be, we could glorify them, without including their ostensible authors. Nor would any true man take exception to this;—least of all, he who writes,—"When the Artist rises high enough to achieve the Beautiful, the symbol by which he makes it perceptible to mortal senses becomes of little value in his eyes, while his spirit possesses itself in the enjoyment of the reality."[27]

---

26 This review by Melville of Hawthorne's collection of stories *Mosses from an Old Manse* (1846) was written soon after the authors first met. It was published in two parts in the *Literary World* on August 17 and 24, 1850. A line of asterisks in the text, which appeared in the original publication, indicates the break between the two days during which Melville wrote the essay.

27 Slightly altered quotation of the last sentence of Hawthorne's story, "The Artist of the Beautiful," which was included in *Mosses from an Old Manse*.

But more than this. I know not what would be the right name to put on the title-page of an excellent book, but this I feel, that the names of all fine authors are fictitious ones, far more than that of Junius,—simply standing, as they do, for the mystical, ever-eluding Spirit of all Beauty, which ubiquitously possesses men of genius. Purely imaginative as this fancy may appear, it nevertheless seems to receive some warranty from the fact, that on a personal interview no great author has ever come up to the idea of his reader. But that dust of which our bodies are composed, how can it fitly express the nobler intelligences among us? With reverence be it spoken, that not even in the case of one deemed more than man, not even in our Saviour, did his visible frame betoken anything of the augustness of the nature within. Else, how could those Jewish eyewitnesses fail to see heaven in his glance.

It is curious, how a man may travel along a country road, and yet miss the grandest, or sweetest of prospects, by reason of an intervening hedge, so like all other hedges, as in no way to hint of the wide landscape beyond. So has it been with me concerning the enchanting landscape in the soul of this Hawthorne, this most excellent Man of Mosses. His "Old Manse" has been written now four years, but I never read it till a day or two since. I had seen it in the book-stores—heard of it often—even had it recommended to me by a tasteful friend, as a rare, quiet book, perhaps too deserving of popularity to be popular. But there are so many books called "excellent", and so much unpopular merit, that amid the thick stir of other things, the hint of my tasteful friend was disregarded; and for four years the Mosses on the old Manse never refreshed me with their perennial green. It may be, however, that all this while, the book, like wine, was only improving in flavor and body. At any rate, it so chanced that this long procrastination eventuated in a happy result. At breakfast the other day, a mountain girl, a cousin of mine, who for the last two weeks has every morning helped me to strawberries and raspberries,—which, like the roses and pearls in the fairy-tale, seemed to fall into the saucer from those strawberry-beds her cheeks,—this delightful creature, this charming Cherry says to me—"I see you spend your mornings in the hay-mow; and yesterday I found there 'Dwight's Travels in New England'. Now I have something far better than that,—something more congenial to our summer on these hills. Take these raspberries, and then I will give you some moss."—"Moss!" said I.—"Yes, and you must take it to the barn with you, and good-bye to 'Dwight'".

With that she left me, and soon returned with a volume, verdantly bound, and garnished with a curious frontispiece in green,—nothing less, than a fragment of real moss cunningly pressed to a fly-leaf.—"Why this," said I spilling my raspberries, "this is the 'Mosses from an Old Manse'". "Yes" said cousin Cherry "yes, it is that flowery Hawthorne."—"Hawthorne and Mosses" said I "no more: it is morning: it is July in the country: and I am off for the barn".

Stretched on that new mown clover, the hill-side breeze blowing over me through the wide barn door, and soothed by the hum of the bees in the meadows around, how magically stole over me this Mossy Man! and how amply, how bountifully, did he redeem that delicious promise to his guests in the Old Manse, of whom it is written—"Others could give them pleasure, or amusement, or instruction—these could be picked up anywhere—but it was for me to give them rest. Rest, in a life of trouble! What better could be done for weary and world-worn spirits? what better could be done for anybody, who came within our magic circle, than to throw the spell of a magic spirit over him?"—So all that day, half-buried in the new clover, I watched this Hawthorne's "Assyrian dawn, and Paphian sunset and moonrise, from the summit of our Eastern Hill."

The soft ravishments of the man spun me round in a web of dreams, and when the book was closed, when the spell was over, this wizard "dismissed me with but misty reminiscences, as if I had been dreaming of him".

What a mild moonlight of contemplative humor bathes that Old Manse!—the rich and rare distilment of a spicy and slowly-oozing heart. No rollicking rudeness, no gross fun fed on fat dinners, and bred in the lees of wine,—but a humor so spiritually gentle, so high, so deep, and yet so richly relishable, that it were hardly inappropriate in an angel. It is the very religion of mirth; for nothing so human but it may be advanced to that. The orchard of the Old Manse seems the visible type of the fine mind that has described it. Those twisted, and contorted old trees, "that stretch out their crooked branches, and take such hold of the imagination, that we remember them as humorists, and odd-fellows." And then, as surrounded by these grotesque forms, and hushed in the noon-day repose of this Hawthorne's spell, how aptly might the still fall of his ruddy thoughts into your soul be symbolized by "the thump of a great apple, in the stillest afternoon, falling without a breath of wind, from the mere necessity of perfect ripeness"! For no less ripe than ruddy are the apples of the thoughts and fancies in this sweet Man of Mosses.

"Buds and Bird-voices"—What a delicious thing is that!—"Will the world ever be so decayed, that Spring may not renew its greenness?"—And the "Fire-Worship". Was ever the hearth so glorified into an altar before? The mere title of that piece is better than any common work in fifty folio volumes. How exquisite is this:—"Nor did it lessen the charm of his soft, familiar courtesy and helpfulness, that the mighty spirit, were opportunity offered him, would run riot through the peaceful house, wrap its inmates in his terrible embrace, and leave nothing of them save their whitened bones. This possibility of mad destruction only made his domestic kindness the more beautiful and touching. It was so sweet of him, being endowed with such power, to dwell, day after day, and one long, lonesome night after another, on the dusky hearth, only now and then betraying his wild nature, by thrusting his red tongue out of the chimney-top! True, he had done much mischief in the world, and was pretty certain to do more, but his warm heart atoned for all. He was kindly to the race of man."

But he has still other apples, not quite so ruddy, though full as ripe;—apples, that have been left to wither on the tree, after the pleasant autumn gathering is past. The sketch of "The Old Apple Dealer" is conceived in the subtlest spirit of sadness; he whose "subdued and nerveless boyhood prefigured his abortive prime, which, likewise, contained within itself the prophecy and image of his lean and torpid age". Such touches as are in this piece can not proceed from any common heart. They argue such a depth of tenderness, such a boundless sympathy with all forms of being, such an omnipresent love, that we must needs say, that this Hawthorne is here almost alone in his generation,—at least, in the artistic manifestation of these things. Still more. Such touches as these,—and many, very many similar ones, all through his chapters—furnish clews, whereby we enter a little way into the intricate, profound heart where they originated. And we see, that suffering, some time or other and in some shape or other,—this only can enable any man to depict it in others. All over him, Hawthorne's melancholy rests like an Indian Summer, which though bathing a whole country in one softness, still reveals the distinctive hue of every towering hill, and each far-winding vale.

But it is the least part of genius that attracts admiration. Where Hawthorne is known, he seems to be deemed a pleasant writer, with a pleasant style,—a sequestered, harmless man, from whom any deep and weighty thing would hardly be anticipated:—a man who means no meanings. But there is no man, in whom humor and love, like mountain peaks, soar to such a rapt height, as to receive the irradiations of the upper skies;—there is no man in whom humor and love are developed in that high form called genius; no such man can exist without also possessing, as the indispensable complement of these, a great, deep intellect, which drops down into the universe like a plummet. Or, love and humor are only the eyes, through which such an intellect views this world. The great beauty in such a mind is but the product of its strength. What, to all readers, can be more charming than the piece entitled "Monsieur du Miroir"; and to a reader at all capable of fully fathoming it, what, at the same time, can possess more mystical depth of meaning?—Yes, there he sits, and looks at me,—this "shape of mystery", this "identical Monsieur du Miroir".—"Methinks I should tremble now, were his wizard power of gliding through all impediments in search of me, to place him suddenly before my eyes".

How profound, nay appalling, is the moral evolved by the "Earth's Holocaust"; where—beginning with the hollow follies and affectations of the world,—all vanities and empty theories and forms, are, one after another, and by an admirably graduated, growing comprehensiveness, thrown into the allegorical fire, till, at length, nothing is left but the all-engendering heart of man; which remaining still unconsumed, the great conflagration is nought.

Of a piece with this, is the "Intelligence Office", a wondrous symbolizing of the secret workings in men's souls. There are other sketches, still more charged with ponderous import.

"The Christmas Banquet", and "The Bosom Serpent" would be fine subjects for a curious and elaborate analysis, touching the conjectural parts of the mind that produced them. For spite of all the Indian-summer sunlight on the hither side of Hawthorne's soul, the other side—like the dark half of the physical sphere—is shrouded in a blackness, ten times black. But this darkness but gives more effect to the ever-moving dawn, that forever advances through it, and circumnavigates his world. Whether Hawthorne has simply availed himself of this mystical blackness as a means to the wondrous effects he makes it to produce in his lights and shades; or whether there really lurks in him, perhaps unknown to himself, a touch of Puritanic gloom,—this, I cannot altogether tell. Certain it is, however, that this great power of blackness in him derives its force from its appeals to that Calvinistic sense of Innate Depravity and Original Sin, from whose visitations, in some shape or other, no deeply thinking mind is always and wholly free. For, in certain moods, no man can weigh this world, without throwing in something, somehow like Original Sin, to strike the uneven balance. At all events, perhaps no writer has ever wielded this terrific thought with greater terror than this same harmless Hawthorne. Still more: this black conceit pervades him, through and through. You may be witched by his sunlight,—transported by the bright gildings in the skies he builds over you;—but there is the blackness of darkness beyond; and even his bright gildings but fringe, and play upon the edges of thunder-clouds.—In one word, the world is mistaken in this Nathaniel Hawthorne. He himself must often have smiled at its absurd misconception of him. He is immeasurably deeper than the plummet of the mere critic. For it is not the brain that can test such a man; it is only the heart. You cannot come to know greatness by inspecting it; there is no glimpse to be caught of it, except by intuition; you need not ring it, you but touch it, and you find it is gold.

Now it is that blackness in Hawthorne, of which I have spoken, that so fixes and fascinates me. It may be, nevertheless, that it is too largely developed in him. Perhaps he does not give us a ray of his light for every shade of his dark. But however this may be, this blackness it is that furnishes the infinite obscure of his background,—that back-ground, against which Shakespeare plays his grandest conceits, the things that have made for Shakespeare his loftiest, but most circumscribed renown, as the profoundest of thinkers. For by philosophers Shakespeare is not adored as the great man of tragedy and comedy.—"Off with his head! so much for Buckingham!" this sort of rant, interlined by another hand, brings down the house,—those mistaken souls, who dream of Shakespeare as a mere man of Richard-the-Third humps, and Macbeth daggers. But it is those deep far-away things in him; those occasional flashings-forth of the intuitive Truth in him; those short, quick probings at the very axis of reality;—these are the things that make Shakespeare, Shakespeare. Through the mouths of the dark characters of Hamlet, Timon, Lear, and Iago, he craftily says, or sometimes insinuates the things, which we feel to be so terrifically true, that it were all but madness for any good man, in his own proper character, to utter, or even hint of them. Tormented into desperation, Lear the frantic King tears off the mask, and speaks the sane madness of vital truth. But, as I before said, it is the least part of genius that attracts admiration. And so, much of the blind, unbridled admiration that has been heaped upon Shakespeare, has been lavished upon the least part of him. And few of his endless commentators and critics seem to have remembered, or even perceived, that the immediate products of a great mind are not so great, as that undeveloped, (and sometimes undevelopable) yet dimly-discernable greatness, to which these immediate products are but the infallible indices. In Shakespeare's tomb lies infinitely more than Shakespeare ever wrote. And if I magnify Shakespeare, it is not so much for what he did do, as for what he did not do, or refrained from doing. For in this world of lies, Truth is forced to fly like a scared white doe in the woodlands; and only by cunning glimpses will she reveal herself, as in Shakespeare and other masters of the great Art of Telling the Truth,—even though it be covertly, and by snatches.

But if this view of the all-popular Shakespeare be seldom taken by his readers, and if very few who extol him, have ever read him deeply, or, perhaps, only have seen him on the tricky stage, (which alone made, and is still making him his mere mob renown)—if few men have time, or patience, or palate, for the spiritual truth as it is in that great genius;—it is, then, no matter of surprise that in a contemporaneous age, Nathaniel Hawthorne is a man, as yet, almost utterly mistaken among men. Here and there, in some quiet arm-chair in the noisy town, or some deep nook among the noiseless mountains, he may be appreciated for something of what he is. But unlike Shakespeare, who was forced to the contrary course by circumstances, Hawthorne (either from simple disinclination, or else from inaptitude) refrains from all the popularizing noise and show of broad farce, and blood-besmeared tragedy; content with the still, rich utterances of a great intellect in repose, and which sends few thoughts into circulation, except they be arterialized at his large warm lungs, and expanded in his honest heart.

Nor need you fix upon that blackness in him, if it suit you not. Nor, indeed, will all readers discern it, for it is, mostly, insinuated to those who may best understand it, and account for it; it is not obtruded upon every one alike.

Some may start to read of Shakespeare and Hawthorne on the same page. They may say, that if an illustration were needed, a lesser light might have sufficed to elucidate this Hawthorne, this small man of yesterday. But I am not, willingly, one of those, who, as touching Shakespeare at least, exemplify the maxim of Rochefoucault, that "we exalt the reputation of some, in order to depress that of others";—who, to teach all noble-souled aspirants that there is no hope for them, pronounce Shakespeare absolutely unapproachable. But Shakespeare has been approached. There are minds that have gone as far as Shakespeare into the universe. And hardly a mortal man, who, at some time or other, has not felt as great thoughts in him as any you will find in Hamlet. We must not inferentially malign mankind for the sake of any one man, whoever he may be. This is too cheap a purchase of contentment for conscious mediocrity to make. Besides, this absolute and unconditional adoration of Shakespeare has grown to be a part of our Anglo Saxon superstitions. The Thirty Nine Articles are now Forty. Intolerance has come to exist in this matter. You must believe in Shakespeare's unapproachability, or quit the country. But what sort of belief is this for an American, a man who is bound to carry republican progressiveness into Literature, as well as into Life? Believe me, my friends, that Shakespeares are this day being born on the banks of the Ohio. And the day will come, when you shall say who reads a book by an Englishman that is a modern? The great mistake seems to be, that even with those Americans who look forward to the coming of a great literary genius among us, they somehow fancy he will come in the costume of Queen Elizabeth's day,—be a writer of dramas founded upon old English history, or the tales of Boccaccio. Whereas, great geniuses are parts of the times; they themselves are the times; and possess a correspondent coloring. It is of a piece with the Jews, who while their Shiloh[28] was meekly walking in their streets, were still praying for his magnificent coming; looking for him in a chariot, who was already among them on an ass. Nor must we forget, that, in his own life-time, Shakespeare was not Shakespeare, but only Master William Shakespeare of the shrewd, thriving, business firm of Condell, Shakespeare & Co., proprietors of the Globe Theatre in London; and by a courtly author, of the name of Greene, was hooted at, as an "upstart crow" beautified "with other birds' feathers". For, mark it well, imitation is often the first charge brought against real originality. Why this is so, there is not space to set forth here. You must have plenty of sea-room to tell the Truth in; especially, when it seems to have an aspect of newness, as America did in 1492, though it was then just as old, and perhaps older than Asia, only those sagacious philosophers, the common sailors, had never seen it before; swearing it was all water and moonshine there.

Now, I do not say that Nathaniel of Salem is a greater than William of Avon, or as great. But the difference between the two men is by no means immeasurable. Not a very great deal more, and Nathaniel were verily William.

This, too, I mean, that if Shakespeare has not been equalled, he is sure to be surpassed, and surpassed by an American born now or yet to be born. For it will never do for us who in most other things out-do as well as out-brag the world, it will not do for us to fold our hands and say, In the highest department advance there is none. Nor will it at all do to say, that the world is getting grey and grizzled now, and has lost that fresh charm which

---

28 Messiah.

she wore of old, and by virtue of which the great poets of past times made themselves what we esteem them to be. Not so. The world is as young today, as when it was created; and this Vermont morning dew is as wet to my feet, as Eden's dew to Adam's. Nor has Nature been all over ransacked by our progenitors, so that no new charms and mysteries remain for this latter generation to find. Far from it. The trillionth part has not yet been said; and all that has been said, but multiplies the avenues to what remains to be said. It is not so much paucity, as superabundance of material that seems to incapacitate modern authors.

Let America then prize and cherish her writers; yea, let her glorify them. They are not so many in number, as to exhaust her good-will. And while she has good kith and kin of her own, to take to her bosom, let her not lavish her embraces upon the household of an alien. For believe it or not England, after all, is, in many things, an alien to us. China has more bowels of real love for us than she. But even were there no Hawthorne, no Emerson, no Whittier, no Irving, no Bryant, no Dana, no Cooper, no Willis (not the author of the "Dashes", but the author of the "Belfry Pigeon")—were there none of these, and others of like calibre among us, nevertheless, let America first praise mediocrity even, in her own children, before she praises (for everywhere, merit demands acknowledgment from every one) the best excellence in the children of any other land. Let her own authors, I say, have the priority of appreciation. I was much pleased with a hot-headed Carolina cousin of mine, who once said,—"If there were no other American to stand by, in Literature,—why, then, I would stand by Pop Emmons and his 'Fredoniad,' and till a better epic came along, swear it was not very far behind the Iliad." Take away the words, and in spirit he was sound.

Not that American genius needs patronage in order to expand.

For that explosive sort of stuff will expand though screwed up in a vice, and burst it, though it were triple steel. It is for the nation's sake, and not for her authors' sake, that I would have America be heedful of the increasing greatness among her writers. For how great the shame, if other nations should be before her, in crowning her heroes of the pen. But this is almost the case now. American authors have received more just and discriminating praise (however loftily and ridiculously given, in certain cases) even from some Englishmen, than from their own countrymen. There are hardly five critics in America; and several of them are asleep. As for patronage, it is the American author who now patronizes his country, and not his country him. And if at times some among them appeal to the people for more recognition, it is not always with selfish motives, but patriotic ones.

It is true, that but few of them as yet have evinced that decided originality which merits great praise. But that graceful writer, who perhaps of all Americans has received the most plaudits from his own country for his productions,—that very popular and amiable writer, however good, and self-reliant in many things, perhaps owes his chief reputation to the self-acknowledged imitation of a foreign model, and to the studied avoidance of all topics but smooth ones. But it is better to fail in originality, than to succeed in imitation. He who has never failed somewhere, that man can not be great. Failure is the true test of greatness. And if it be said, that continual success is a proof that a man wisely knows his powers,—it is only to be added, that, in that case, he knows them to be small. Let us believe it, then, once for all, that there is no hope for us in these smooth pleasing writers that know their powers. Without malice, but to speak the plain fact, they but furnish an appendix to Goldsmith, and other English authors. And we want no American Goldsmiths; nay, we want no American Miltons. It were the vilest thing you could say of a true American author, that he were an American Tompkins. Call him an American, and have done; for you can not say a nobler thing of him.—But it is not meant that all American writers should studiously cleave to nationality in their writings; only this, no American writer should write like an Englishman, or a Frenchman; let him write like a man, for then he will be sure to write like an American. Let us away with this Bostonian leaven of literary flunkeyism towards England. If either must play the flunkey in this thing, let England do it, not us. And the time is not far off when circumstances may force her to it. While we are rapidly preparing for that political supremacy among the nations, which prophetically awaits us at the close of the present century; in a literary point of view, we are deplorably unprepared for it; and we seem studious to remain so. Hitherto, reasons might have existed why this should be; but no good reason exists now. And all that is requisite to amendment in this matter, is simply this: that, while freely acknowledging all excellence, everywhere, we should refrain from unduly lauding foreign writers and, at the same time, duly recognize the meritorious writers that are our own;—those writers, who breathe that unshackled, democratic spirit of Christianity in all things, which now takes the practical lead in the world, though at the same time led by ourselves—us Americans. Let us boldly contemn all imitation, though it comes to us graceful and fragrant as the morning; and foster all originality, though, at first, it be crabbed and ugly as our own pine knots. And if any of our authors fail, or seem to fail, then, in the words of my enthusiastic Carolina cousin, let us clap him on the shoulder, and back him against all Europe for his second round. The truth is, that in our point of view, this matter of a national literature has come to such a pass with us, that in some sense we must turn bullies, else the day is lost, or superiority so far beyond us, that we can hardly say it will ever be ours.

And now, my countrymen, as an excellent author, of your own flesh and blood,—an unimitating, and, perhaps, in his way, an inimitable man—whom better can I commend to you, in the first place, than Nathaniel Hawthorne. He is one of the new, and far better generation of your writers. The smell of your beeches and hemlocks is upon him; your own broad prairies are in his soul; and if you travel away inland into his deep and noble nature, you will hear the far roar of his Niagara. Give not over to future generations the glad duty of acknowledging him for what he is. Take that joy to your self, in your own generation; and so shall he feel those grateful impulses in him, that may possibly prompt him to the full flower of some still greater achievement in your eyes. And by confessing him, you thereby confess others; you brace the whole brotherhood. For genius, all over the world, stands hand in hand, and one shock of recognition runs the whole circle round.

In treating of Hawthorne, or rather of Hawthorne in his writings (for I never saw the man; and in the chances of a quiet plantation life, remote from his haunts, perhaps never shall[29]) in treating of his works, I say, I have thus far omitted all mention of his "Twice Told Tales", and "Scarlet Letter".[30] Both are excellent; but full of such manifold, strange and diffusive beauties, that time would all but fail me, to point the half of them out. But there are things in those two books, which, had they been written in

29 Melville was not telling the truth here; he had met Hawthorne just a few days before he wrote this essay. His motivations for hiding this fact are unclear, though he may have wanted his praise of Hawthorne to appear more objective than would otherwise have been the case.

30 Hawthorne's collection *Twice-Told Tales* was first published in 1837. An expanded edition came out in 1842. *The Scarlet Letter*, widely considered to be Hawthorne's masterpiece, was published in 1850.

England a century ago, Nathaniel Hawthorne had utterly displaced many of the bright names we now revere on authority. But I am content to leave Hawthorne to himself, and to the infallible finding of posterity; and however great may be the praise I have bestowed upon him, I feel, that in so doing, I have more served and honored myself, than him. For, at bottom, great excellence is praise enough to itself; but the feeling of a sincere and appreciative love and admiration towards it, this is relieved by utterance; and warm, honest praise ever leaves a pleasant flavor in the mouth; and it is an honorable thing to confess to what is honorable in others.

But I cannot leave my subject yet. No man can read a fine author, and relish him to his very bones, while he reads, without subsequently fancying to himself some ideal image of the man and his mind. And if you rightly look for it, you will almost always find that the author himself has somewhere furnished you with his own picture.—For poets (whether in prose or verse), being painters of Nature, are like their brethren of the pencil, the true portrait-painters, who, in the multitude of likenesses to be sketched, do not invariably omit their own; and in all high instances, they paint them without any vanity, though, at times, with a lurking something, that would take several pages to properly define.

I submit it, then, to those best acquainted with the man personally, whether the following is not Nathaniel Hawthorne;—and to himself, whether something involved in it does not express the temper of his mind,—that lasting temper of all true, candid men—a seeker, not a finder yet:—

> "A man now entered, in neglected attire, with the aspect of a thinker, but somewhat too rough-hewn and

> brawny for a scholar. His face was full of sturdy vigor, with some finer and keener attribute beneath; though harsh at first, it was tempered with the glow of a large, warm heart, which had force enough to heat his powerful intellect through and through. He advanced to the Intelligencer, and looked at him with a glance of such stern sincerity, that perhaps few secrets were beyond its scope.
>
> "'I seek for Truth', said he."

* * * * *

Twenty-four hours have elapsed since writing the foregoing. I have just returned from the hay mow, charged more and more with love and admiration of Hawthorne. For I have just been gleaning through the Mosses, picking up many things here and there that had previously escaped me. And I found that but to glean after this man, is better than to be in at the harvest of others. To be frank (though, perhaps, rather foolish) notwithstanding what I wrote yesterday of these Mosses, I had not then culled them all; but had, nevertheless, been sufficiently sensible of the subtle essence, in them, as to write as I did. To what infinite height of loving wonder and admiration I may yet be borne, when by repeatedly banquetting on these Mosses, I shall have thoroughly incorporated their whole stuff into my being,—that, I can not tell. But already I feel that this Hawthorne has dropped germinous seeds into my soul. He expands and deepens down, the more I contemplate him; and further, and further, shoots his strong New-England roots into the hot soil of my Southern soul.

By careful reference to the "Table of Contents", I now find, that I have gone through all the sketches; but that when I yesterday wrote, I had not at all read two particular pieces, to which I now desire to call special attention,—"A Select Party", and

"Young Goodman Brown". Here, be it said to all those whom this poor fugitive scrawl of mine may tempt to the perusal of the "Mosses," that they must on no account suffer themselves to be trifled with, disappointed, or deceived by the triviality of many of the titles to these Sketches. For in more than one instance, the title utterly belies the piece. It is as if rustic demijohns containing the very best and costliest of Falernian and Tokay, were labeled "Cider", "Perry," and "Elderberry wine". The truth seems to be, that like many other geniuses, this Man of Mosses takes great delight in hoodwinking the world,—at least, with respect to himself. Personally, I doubt not, that he rather prefers to be generally esteemed but a so-so sort of author; being willing to reserve the thorough and acute appreciation of what he is, to that party most qualified to judge—that is, to himself. Besides, at the bottom of their natures, men like Hawthorne, in many things, deem the plaudits of the public such strong presumptive evidence of mediocrity in the object of them, that it would in some degree render them doubtful of their own powers, did they hear much and vociferous braying concerning them in the public pastures. True, I have been braying myself (if you please to be witty enough, to have it so) but then I claim to be the first that has so brayed in this particular matter; and therefore, while pleading guilty to the charge still claim all the merit due to originality.

But with whatever motive, playful or profound, Nathaniel Hawthorne has chosen to entitle his pieces in the manner he has, it is certain, that some of them are directly calculated to deceive—egregiously deceive, the superficial skimmer of pages. To be downright and candid once more, let me cheerfully say, that two of these titles did dolefully dupe no less an eagle-eyed reader than myself; and that, too, after I had been impressed with a sense of the great depth and breadth of this American man.

"Who in the name of thunder" (as the country-people say in this neighborhood) "who in the name of thunder", would anticipate any marvel in a piece entitled "Young Goodman Brown"? You would of course suppose that it was a simple little tale, intended as a supplement to "Goody Two Shoes". Whereas, it is deep as Dante; nor can you finish it, without addressing the author in his own words—"It is yours to penetrate, in every bosom, the deep mystery of sin". And with Young Goodman, too, in allegorical pursuit of his Puritan wife, you cry out in your anguish,—

> "'Faith!' shouted Goodman Brown, in a voice of agony and desperation; and the echoes of the forest mocked him, crying—'Faith! Faith!' as if bewildered wretches were seeking her all through the wilderness."

Now this same piece, entitled "Young Goodman Brown", is one of the two that I had not all read yesterday; and I allude to it now, because it is, in itself, such a strong positive illustration of that blackness in Hawthorne, which I had assumed from the mere occasional shadows of it, as revealed in several of the other sketches. But had I previously perused "Young Goodman Brown", I should have been at no pains to draw the conclusion, which I came to, at a time, when I was ignorant that the book contained one such direct and unqualified manifestation of it.

The other piece of the two referred to, is entitled "A Select Party", which, in my first simplicity upon originally taking hold of the book, I fancied must treat of some pumpkin-pie party in Old Salem, or some chowder party on Cape Cod. Whereas, by all the gods of Peedee![31] it is the sweetest and sublimest thing that has been written since Spenser wrote. Nay, there is nothing in

31 The Pedee (or Pee Dee or Great Pee Dee) River flows through North and South Carolina.

Spenser that surpasses it, perhaps, nothing that equals it. And the test is this: read any canto in "The Faery Queen", and then read "A Select Party", and decide which pleases you the most,—that is, if you are qualified to judge. Do not be frightened at this; for when Spenser was alive, he was thought of very much as Hawthorne is now,—was generally accounted just such a "gentle" harmless man. It may be, that to common eyes, the sublimity of Hawthorne seems lost in his sweetness,—as perhaps in this same "Select Party" of his; for whom, he has builded so august a dome of sunset clouds, and served them on richer plate, than Belshazzar's when he banquetted his lords in Babylon.[32]

But my chief business now, is to point out a particular page in this piece, having reference to an honored guest, who under the name of "The Master Genius" but in the guise of "a young man of poor attire, with no insignia of rank or acknowledged eminence", is introduced to the Man of Fancy, who is the giver of the feast. Now the page having reference to this "Master Genius", so happily expresses much of what I yesterday wrote, touching the coming of the literary Shiloh of America, that I cannot but be charmed by the coincidence; especially, when it shows such a parity of ideas, at least, in this one point, between a man like Hawthorne and a man like me.

And here, let me throw out another conceit of mine touching this American Shiloh, or "Master Genius", as Hawthorne calls him. May it not be, that this commanding mind has not been, is not, and never will be, individually developed in any one man? And would it, indeed, appear so unreasonable to suppose, that this great fullness and overflowing may be, or may be destined to

---

32 Belshazzar (?-539 B.C.) ruled Babylon under his father, Nabonidus. Chapter 5 of the Book of Daniel begins, "Belshazzar the king made a great feast to a thousand of his lords, and drank wine before the thousand" (King James Version).

be, shared by a plurality of men of genius? Surely, to take the very greatest example on record, Shakespeare cannot be regarded as in himself the concretion of all the genius of his time; nor as so immeasurably beyond Marlow, Webster, Ford, Beaumont, Jonson, that those great men can be said to share none of his power? For one, I conceive that there were dramatists in Elizabeth's day, between whom and Shakespeare the distance was by no means great. Let anyone, hitherto little acquainted with those neglected old authors, for the first time read them thoroughly, or even read Charles Lamb's Specimens of them, and he will be amazed at the wondrous ability of those Anaks of men,[33] and shocked at this renewed example of the fact, that Fortune has more to do with fame than merit,—though, without merit, lasting fame there can be none.

Nevertheless, it would argue too illy of my country were this maxim to hold good concerning Nathaniel Hawthorne, a man, who already, in some few minds, has shed "such a light, as never illuminates the earth, save when a great heart burns as the household fire of a grand intellect."

The words are his,—in the "Select Party"; and they are a magnificent setting to a coincident sentiment of my own, but ramblingly expressed yesterday, in reference to himself. Gainsay it who will, as I now write, I am Posterity speaking by proxy—and after times will make it more than good, when I declare—that the American, who up to the present day, has evinced, in Literature, the largest brain with the largest heart, that man is Nathaniel Hawthorne. Moreover, that whatever Nathaniel Hawthorne may hereafter write, "The Mosses from an Old

---

33 Giants. The last verse of chapter 13 of the Book of Numbers reads, "And there we saw the giants, the sons of Anak, which come of the giants: and we were in our own sight as grasshoppers, and so we were in their sight" (King James Version).

Manse" will be ultimately accounted his masterpiece. For there is a sure, though a secret sign in some works which proves the culmination of the powers (only the developable ones, however) that produced them. But I am by no means desirous of the glory of a prophet. I pray Heaven that Hawthorne may *yet* prove me an impostor in this prediction. Especially, as I somehow cling to the strange fancy, that, in all men, hiddenly reside certain wondrous, occult properties—as in some plants and minerals—which by some happy but very rare accident (as bronze was discovered by the melting of the iron and brass in the burning of Corinth) may chance to be called forth here on earth; not entirely waiting for their better discovery in the more congenial, blessed atmosphere of heaven.

Once more—for it is hard to be finite upon an infinite subject, and all subjects are infinite. By some people, this entire scrawl of mine may be esteemed altogether unnecessary, inasmuch, "as years ago" (they may say) "we found out the rich and rare stuff in this Hawthorne, whom you now parade forth, as if only *yourself* were the discoverer of this Portuguese diamond in our Literature".—But even granting all this; and adding to it, the assumption that the books of Hawthorne have sold by the five-thousand,—what does that signify?—They should be sold by the hundred-thousand; and read by the million; and admired by every one who is capable of admiration.

from CLAREL: A POEM AND PILGRIMAGE IN THE HOLY LAND[34]

(1876)

PART 2, THE WILDERNESS

Canto 27, Vine and Clarel

While now, to serve the pilgrim train,
The Arabs willow branches hew,
(For palms they serve in dearth of true),
Or, kneeling by the margin, stoop
To brim memorial bottles up;
And the Greek's wine entices two:
Apart see Clarel here incline,
Perplexed by that Dominican,
Nor less by Rolfe—capricious man:
"I cannot penetrate him.—Vine?"
    As were Venetian slats between,
He espied him through a leafy screen,
Luxurious there in umbrage thrown,
Light sprays above his temples blown—
The river through the green retreat
Hurrying, reveling by his feet.
    Vine looked an overture, but said
Nothing, till Clarel leaned—half laid—
Beside him: then "We dream, or be

34 *Clarel: A Poem and Pilgrimage in the Holy Land* was first published in 1876 by G. P. Putnam's Sons. The poem is inscribed to Peter Gansevoort, Melville's uncle, who subsidized the publication of the work.

In sylvan John's baptistery:
May Pisa's equal beauty keep?—
But how bad habits persevere!
I have been moralizing here
Like any imbecile: as thus:
Look how these willows over-weep
The waves, and plain: 'Fleet so from us?
And wherefore? whitherward away?
Your best is here where wildings sway
And the light shadow's blown about;
Ah, tarry, for at hand's a sea
Whence ye shall never issue out
Once in.' They sing back: 'So let be!
We mad-caps hymn it as we flow—
Short life and merry! be it so!'"
 Surprised at such a fluent turn,
The student did but listen—learn.

 Putting aside the twigs which screened,
Again Vine spake, and lightly leaned
"Look; in yon vault so leafy dark,
At deep end lit by gemmy spark
Of mellowed sunbeam in a snare;
Over the stream—ay, just through there—
The sheik on that celestial mare
Shot, fading.—Clan of outcast Hagar,
Well do ye come by spear and dagger!
Yet in your bearing ye outvie
Our western Red Men, chiefs that stalk
In mud paint—whirl the tomahawk.—
But in these Nimrods noted you

The natural language of the eye,
Burning or liquid, flame or dew,
As still the changeable quick mood
Made transit in the wayward blood?
Methought therein one might espy,
For all the wildness, thoughts refined
By the old Asia's dreamful mind;
But hark—a bird?"
                                        Pure as the rain
Which diamondeth with lucid grain,
The white swan in the April hours
Floating between two sunny showers
Upon the lake, while buds unroll;
So pure, so virginal in shrine
Of true unworldliness looked Vine.
Ah, clear sweet ether of the soul
(Mused Clarel), holding him in view.
Prior advances unreturned
Not here he recked of, while he yearned—
O, now but for communion true
And close; let go each alien theme;
Give me thyself!
                                        But Vine, at will
Dwelling upon his wayward dream,
Nor as suspecting Clarel's thrill
Of personal longing, rambled still;
"Methinks they show a lingering trace
Of some quite unrecorded race
Such as the Book of Job implies.
What ages of refinings wise
Must have forerun what there is writ—

More ages than have followed it.
At Lydda late, as chance would have,
Some tribesmen from the south I saw,
Their tents pitched in the Gothic nave,
The ruined one. Disowning law,
Not lawless lived they; no, indeed;
Their chief—why, one of Sydney's clan,
A slayer, but chivalric man;
And chivalry, with all that breed
Was Arabic or Saracen
In source, they tell. But, as men stray
Further from Ararat away
Pity it were did they recede
In carriage, manners, and the rest;
But no, for ours the palm indeed
In bland amenities far West!
Come now, for pastime let's complain;
Grudged thanks, Columbus, for thy main!
Put back, as 'twere—assigned by fate
To fight crude Nature o'er again,
By slow degrees we re-create.
But then, alas, in Arab camps
No lack, they say, no lack of scamps."
    Divided mind knew Clarel here;
The heart's desire did interfere.
Thought he, How pleasant in another
Such sallies, or in thee, if said
After confidings that should wed
Our souls in one:—Ah, call me *brother!*—
So feminine his passionate mood
Which, long as hungering unfed,

All else rejected or withstood.
  Some inklings he let fall. But no:
Here over Vine there slid a change—
A shadow, such as thin may show
Gliding along the mountain-range
And deepening in the gorge below.
  Does Vine's rebukeful dusking say—
Why, on this vernal bank to-day,
Why bring oblations of thy pain
To one who hath his share? here fain
Would lap him in a chance reprieve?
Lives none can help ye; that believe.
Art thou the first soul tried by doubt?
Shalt prove the last? Go, live it out.
But for thy fonder dream of love
In man toward man—the soul's caress—
The negatives of flesh should prove
Analogies of non-cordialness
In spirit.—E'en such conceits could cling
To Clarel's dream of vain surmise
And imputation full of sting.
But, glancing up, unwarned he saw
What serious softness in those eyes
Bent on him. Shyly they withdraw.
Enslaver, wouldst thou but fool me
With bitter-sweet, sly sorcery,
Pride's pastime? or wouldst thou indeed,
Since things unspoken may impede,
Let flow thy nature but for bar?—

Nay, dizzard,[35] sick these feelings are;
How findest place within thy heart
For such solicitudes apart
From Ruth?[36]—Self-taxings.

But a sign
Came here indicative from Vine,
Who with a reverent hushed air
His view directed toward the glade
Beyond, wherein a niche was made
Of leafage, and a kneeler there,
The meek one, on whom, as he prayed,
A golden shaft of mellow light,
Oblique through vernal cleft above,
And making his pale forehead bright,
Scintillant fell. By such a beam
From heaven descended erst the dove
On Christ emerging from the stream.
It faded; 'twas a transient ray;
And, quite unconscious of its sheen,
The suppliant rose and moved away,
Not dreaming that he had been seen.

When next they saw that innocent,
From prayer such cordial had he won
That all his aspect of content
As with the oil of gladness shone.
Less aged looked he. And his cheer

---

35 Foolish fellow, idiot.

36 Clarel meets Ruth in Jerusalem and falls in love with her. She later dies of grief upon hearing the news of her father's drowning.

Took language in an action here:
The train now mustering in line,
Each pilgrim with a river-palm
In hand (except indeed the Jew),
The saint the head-stall need entwine
With wreathage of the same. When new
They issued from the wood, no charm
The ass found in such idle gear
Superfluous: with her long ear
She flapped it off, and the next thrust
Of hoof imprinted it in dust.
Meek hands (mused Vine), vainly ye twist
Fair garland for the realist.
    The Hebrew, noting whither bent
Vine's glance, a word in passing lent:
"Ho, tell us how it comes to be
That thou who rank'st not with beginners
Regard have for yon chief of sinners."
    "Yon chief of sinners?"
                                        "So names he
Himself. For one I'll not express
How I do loathe such lowliness."

MONODY[37]

(1891)

To have known him, to have loved him,
    After loneness long;
And then to be estranged in life,
    And neither in the wrong;
And now for death to set his seal—
    Ease me, a little ease, my song!

By wintry hills his hermit-mound
    The sheeted snow-drifts drape,
And houseless there the snow-bird flits
    Beneath the fir-tree's crape:
Glazed now with ice the cloistral vine
    That hid the shyest grape.

---

37 "Monody" was first published by Caxton Press as part of Melville's collection of poems entitled *Timoleon Etc.* in 1891, the year of his death.

APPENDIX

John H. Clifford's Narrative Account of the Story of Agatha[38]

MAY 28TH 1842 Saturday. I have just returned from a visit to Falmouth with a Mr Janney of Mo on one of the most interesting and romantic cases I ever expect to be engaged in.—The gentleman from Missouri Mr Janney came to my house last Sunday Evening and related to myself and partner that he had married the daughter of a Mrs Irvin formerly of Pittsburgh Pa. and that Mrs Irvin had married a second husband by the name of Robertson. The latter deceased about two years since He was appointed Admr to his Estate which amounted to $20 000—about 15 months afterwards Mrs Robertson also died and in the meantime the Admr had been engaged in looking up heirs to the Estate—He learned that Robertson was an Englishman whose original name was Shinn—that he resided at Alexandria D.C. where he had two nephews—He also wrote to England and had ascertained the history and genealogy of the family with much accuracy, when on going to the Post Office one day he found a letter directed to James Robertson the deceased, post marked Falmouth Massstts On opening it he found it from a person signing herself Rebecca A. Gifford and addressing him as "Father." The existence of this girl had been known before by Mrs Robertson and her husband had pronounced her to be illegitimate The Admr then addressed a letter to Mrs Gifford informing her of the

38 This narrative, in the form of a clerk's transcription, was enclosed with Melville's letter to Hawthorne of August 13, 1852.

decease of her father. He was surprized soon after by the appearance in S[t] Louis of a shrewd Quaker from Falmouth named Dillingham with full powers and fortified by letters and affidavits shewing the existence of a wife in Falmouth whom Robertson married in 1807 at Pembroke Mss & the legitimacy of the daughter who had married a M[r] Gifford and laying strong claims to the entire property.

The Adm[r] and heirs having strong doubts arising from the declarations of Robertson during his lifetime & the peculiar expressions contained in the letters exhibited, as to the validity of the marriage & the claim based upon it, determined to resist and legal proceedings were at once commenced. The object of the visit of M[r] Janney was to attend the taking of depositions, upon a notice from the claimants—The Minister Town Clerk and Witnesses present at the ceremony established the fact of a legal marriage and the birth of a child in wedlock, beyond all cavil or controversy all of the witnesses were of the highest respectability and the widow and daughter interested me very much.

It appeared that Robertson was wrecked on the coast of Pembroke where this girl, then Miss Agatha Hatch was living—that he was hospitably entertained and cared for, and that within a year after, he married her, in due form of law—that he went two short voyages to sea. About two years after the marriage, leaving his wife *enciente* he started off in search of employment and from that time until *Seventeen* years afterwards she never heard from him in any way whatsoever, directly or indirectly, not even a word. Being poor she went out nursing for her daily bread and yet contrived out of her small earnings to give her daughter a first rate education. Having become connected with the Society of Friends she sent her to their most celebrated boarding school and when I saw her I found she had profited by all her advantages beyond most females. In the meantime Robertson had gone to Alexandria D.C. where he had entered into a successful and profitable business and married a second wife. At the expiration of this long period of 17 years which for the poor forsaken wife, had glided wearily away, while she was engaged away from home, her Father rode up in a gig and informed her that her husband had returned and wished to see her and her child—but if she would not see him, to see her child at all events—They all returned together and encountered him on the way coming to meet them about half a mile from her father's house. This meeting was described to me by the mother and daughter—Every incident seemed branded upon the memories of both. He excused himself as well as he could for his long absence and silence, appeared very affectionate refused to tell where he was living and persuaded them not to make any inquiries, gave them a handsome sum of money, promised to return for good and left the next day—He appeared again in about a year, just on the eve of his daughter's marriage & gave her a bridal present. It was not long after this that his wife in Alexandria died—He then wrote to his son-in-law to come there—He did so—remained 2 days and brought back a gold watch and three handsome shawls which had been previously worn by some person—They all admitted that they had suspicions then & from this circumstance that he had been a second time married.

Soon after this he visited Falmouth again & as it proved for the last time—He announced his intention of removing to Missouri & urged the whole family to go with him, promising money land and other assistance to his son-in-law. The offer was not accepted He shed tears when he bade them farewell—From the time of his return to Missouri till the time of his death a constant correspondence was kept up money was remitted by him annually and he announced to them his marriage with Mrs Irvin—He had no children by either of his last two wives.

Mr Janney was entirely disappointed in the character of the evidence and the character of the claimants. He considered them, when he first came, as parties to the imposition practised upon Mrs Irvin & her children. But I was satisfied and I think he was, that their motives in keeping silence were high and pure, creditable in every way to the true Mrs Robertson.

She stated the causes with a simplicity & pathos which carried that conviction irresistibly to my mind. The only good(?) it could have done to expose him would have been to drive Robertson away and forever disgrace him & it would certainly have made Mrs Irvin & her children wretched for the rest of their days—"I had no wish" said the wife "to make either of them unhappy, notwithstanding all I had suffered on his account"—It was to me a most striking instance of long continued & uncomplaining submission to wrong and anguish on the part of a wife, wch made her in my eyes a heroine.

Janney informed me that R. and his last wife did not live very happily together and particularly that he seemed to be a very jealous suspicious man—That when a person called at his house he would never enter the room till he knew who it was & "all about him. He must have recieved a portion of his punishment in this life. The fact came out in the course of examination that they had agreed to give Dillingham one half of what he might obtain deducting the expenses from his half—After the strength of the evidence became known Mr Janney commenced the making of serious efforts to effect a compromise of the claim What the result will be time will shew—This is, I suspect, the end of my connexion with the case—

New Bedford July 14th 1852

Herman Melville
Dr Sir

Above I send you the little story I promised you—

Respectfully Yours.

P.S. The business was settled in a few weeks afterwards, in a most amicable & honorable manner, by a division of the property. I think Mrs. Robinson & her family refused to claim or receive anything that really belonged to Mrs. Irwin, or which Robinson had derived through her.—

ABOUT THE CONTRIBUTORS

MARK NIEMEYER is professor of American literature and American history at the Université de Bourgogne in Dijon, France. His research focuses on nineteenth-century writings of the antebellum period and is frequently concerned with questions related to cultural nationalism and national identity. He has published numerous articles and is co-editor of several editions of works by Herman Melville, including the French "Folio Classique" edition of *Mardi* (2011), the Norton Critical edition of *The Confidence-Man* (2005), and the French "Pléiade" editions of *Mardi* (1997) and *Moby-Dick* (2006). He has also served as a contributing scholar on the Northwestern-Newberry editions of *Moby-Dick* (1988) and *Clarel* (1991). He is co-editor of *Literature on the Move: Comparing Diasporic Ethnicities in Europe and the Americas* (2002) and co-author of an American and British history textbook for French students, *Repères de civilisation: Grande-Bretagne, Etats-Unis* (2003). Niemeyer has also published illustrated works of general interest including *Water: The Essence of Life* (2008) and *Wonders of the World: World of Man* (2010).

PAUL HARDING is the author of two novels about multiple generations of a New England family: *Tinkers* (recipient of the 2010 Pulitzer Prize) and *Enon*. A graduate of the University of Massachusetts, he was a drummer for the band Cold Water Flat before earning his MFA from the Iowa Writers' Workshop. Harding has also received a Guggenheim Fellowship and was a fiction fellow at the Fine Arts Center in Provincetown. He lives in Massachusetts with his wife and two sons.

ABOUT ORISON BOOKS

Orison Books is a 501(c)3 non-profit literary press focused on the life of the spirit from a broad and inclusive range of perspectives. We seek to publish books of exceptional poetry, fiction, and non-fiction from perspectives spanning the spectrum of spiritual and religious thought, ethnicity, gender identity, and sexual orientation.

As a non-profit literary press, Orison Books depends on the support of donors. To find out more about our mission and our books, or to make a donation, please visit www.orisonbooks.com.